FOR THOSE ABOUT TO ROCK

A Road Map to Being in a Band

DAVE BIDINI

Tundra Books

Chapter-opening graphic © Martin Tielli

Published in Canada by Tundra Books,
481 University Avenue, Toronto, Ontario M5G 2E9

Published in the United States by Tundra Books of Northern New York,
P.O. Box 1030, Plattsburgh, New York 12901

Library of Congress Control Number: 2004105081

National Library of Canada Cataloguing in Publication

Bidini, Dave
    For those about to rock : a road map to being in a band /
Dave Bidini.

Includes index.
ISBN 0-88776-653-6

    1. Rock music – Vocational guidance – Canada – Juvenile literature.
2. Music trade – Canada – Juvenile literature. I. Title.

ML3795.B585 2004   J781.64'023'71   C2004-902208-3

We acknowledge the financial support of the Government of Canada
through the Book Publishing Industry Development Program
(BPIDP) and that of the Government of Ontario through the Ontario
Media Development Corporation's Ontario Book Initiative. We further
acknowledge the support of the Canada Council for the Arts and the
Ontario Arts Council for our publishing program.

Design: Cindy Reichle

Printed and bound in Canada

This book is printed on acid-free paper that is 100% recycled,
ancient-forest friendly (40% post-consumer recycled).

1 2 3 4 5 6   09 08 07 06 05 04

For my sister

Contents

Introduction

Let There Be Rock

I'm forty years old as I write this. I hope that sounds old. If it doesn't sound old to you, then you're my peer, my equal, my generational brother or sister. If that's the case, you have no right reading this book. It isn't for you. It's for those who wouldn't be caught dead sitting next to you on the bus. So, if you don't mind? There. Now go busy yourself with some shuffleboard or something.

Sorry about that. Believe me, it's just as maddening when they open books not meant for them as it is when they burst into your room uninvited. Anyway, like I was saying: I am old. Not Yoda old or Gollum old. Not wool-socked, suspendered, Hush Puppied, spearmint-gummed,

EZ-Rocked, rye-and-whiskeyed old, mind you. But still:
old. Bluesman old. I'm old in that I've ingested enough
rock and roll over the course of my life that the *skree*ing at
the back of my hearing recalls countless hours spent with
my right ear tipped to the tweeter of my Mesa Boogie amp
combo, scraping an A–G–D chord progression against the
pick guard of a gravy-brown MusicMan StingRay II guitar
with all the poise of a dog scratching its flea-bitten hind. It
recalls moments spent blasting whatever tape deck/CD
player/8-track/AM/FM radio contraption was rigged to
whatever car I was riding in at the time, to say nothing of
the parade of rumbling rented vans that my band – the
Rheostatics – have driven across the snow-clawed
highways of Canada, digging the beauty of a big
telegraphed chorus, or a ten-minute guitar freak-out, or a
gaunt singer's howl in hopes of maintaining the flickering
fire of youth, which continues to burn, if not roar – unlike
those who've succumbed to the dappling candlelight of
adulthood, whom I've already told to get lost, but, you
know, some people . . .

Back in the day when I was nothing but a pimply little
question mark, there were very few books that talked about
what it meant to be a musician. These books might have
existed, but they never made it to the suburbs, to
Etobicoke, which is where I grew up with my parents,

younger sister, and dog. As a kid, I read every book that had anything even remotely to do with rock and roll; most were as thin as a Saltine cracker. Back then, I had yet to catch on to books like *Espedair Street* by Iain Banks, or *A Drink with Shane MacGowan*, the singer for the Pogues, or *Heart Like a Wheel* by the Band's Levon Helm, or *Please Kill Me: The Uncensored Oral History of Punk* by Legs MacNeil and Gillian McCain, or *Whale Music* by Paul Quarrington, all of which I've since devoured as a frosty-top. Instead I filled my cranium with unprobing pop biographies of Eric Clapton, Robert Plant, Queen, and Alice Cooper. In Alice's book, he talked about dousing hotel lobbies with fire extinguishers, dressing in bejeweled pajamas, and rigging bogus guillotines on stage. Otherwise, the Coop and his peers never said what rock and roll smelled, tasted, or felt like. It wasn't until my local Smoke and Gift shop at Westway Plaza started getting *Hit Parader*, *Creem*, and *Rolling Stone* magazines (each of which hit their creative height with the rise of Punk in the late 1970s, just around the time I became a teenager) that I was turned on to true stories about the lives of the rock gods whose music filled – and continues to fill – my every waking moment.

I remember a book from the library at Dixon Grove Middle School: *Getting Ahead in the Music Business*. No matter how many times I read it, it made little sense to me.

There was lots of talk about management, lawyers, accountants, promoters, agents, record labels, and copyright – words that seemed to be the opposite of the ones that grabbed me: fuzztone, T-Wah, floor tom, slapback, hammer-on, and finger-tap. *Getting Ahead* was about as wild and entrancing as a Sears catalog. The cover photo showed a guitarist with medium-length hair, styled cautiously below the ear, giving the camera a wary look as he leaned against a mixing console. He possessed all the kinetic energy and crazy buzz of a yellow Yield sign.

So, when it was suggested to me that I take a stab at creating the kind of book that hadn't existed when I'd lock myself in my room for hours trying to figure out the difference between A7 and A7-diminished chords – a task I ultimately abandoned to make whooping noises out of my guitar's F-holes – I told the publisher that I'd give it a try. Since I've always thought that part of the fun of rock and roll is finding your own way, I'll attempt, over the next handful of chapters, not to say too much instead of bludgeoning you with *Do*s and *Don't*s. In rock and roll (and art in general), there's no right or wrong way to do things. If there was, Mississippi Fred MacDowell never would have pioneered bottleneck guitar by sliding an old chicken bone up and down the neck; Larry Graham wouldn't have invented slap bass as a rhythmic substitute for drummer

Greg Errico, who called in sick for band practice with Sly and the Family Stone; and Neil Young never would have found his sound after plugging in an amp that had just plummeted down a flight of stairs. The Beatles never would have hired Ringo, and old Moulty – the one-handed surf drummer for the Barbarians – would have never picked up a set of sticks. There are very few maxims in art – though I've always felt that Geddy Lee's "Always bring your wallet with you on stage" is fairly sage advice – so I'll resist the urge to preach about what it takes to put out twelve albums, record the odd hit single, or embark on twenty years of touring, as I have with the Rheos, who never knew what we were doing half the time, anyway.

I've tried to organize these chapters to touch on the very basics about what it means to be a musician, and, even then, I'm not exactly sure what they are. A musician is someone who plays in basements and hockey rinks, at weddings or papal events. Every player, from Bono to your Uncle Bob, first approached their instrument of choice as if it were a coiled viper, dangerous to the touch. It might seem as if Bruce Springsteen, or John Lennon, or Bob Dylan, or Dylan Hudecki (I throw my friend Dylan in here to make the point) strode on to the world's stage fully formed, but they too went through all of those things that you're going through (or are about to go through) as a musician, all of those doubts and fears and uncertainties and trepidation and parental pressure and peer taunting and betrayal of the heart. Like you, they were also bitten by the bug, singing and playing and writing in an effort to make sense of all of their difficult thoughts and emotions.

Rik Emmett, of the hard-rock band Triumph (Rik dropped the c in his name after it was misprinted on an album), once told me, "There are two kinds of musicians: Those who *want* to play, and those who *have* to play." If anything comes from the sweat and blood and sore wrists that occurred during the writing of this book – truth be told, I'm drinking a coffee and munching on a cruller as I pin down this very thought – it's that you'll have decided what kind of musician you are, and what kind you want to be. But if you don't or can't, don't worry either. Rock and roll is a most serious and important thing, but it's also stupid, stupid fun. If you get tickled somewhere between those two places, you'll be all right.

Now, lets kick out those jams, shall we?

The Mythology of Making It

And the Fickle Fruit of Fame

Now that we've established that there's no real wrong or right way of approaching rock and roll (though plugging your new guitar into a wall socket, as an elderly patron of my local music store once did – that is wrong), we should probably address what people mean by "making it." If you've come to this book as a rock-star-in-waiting, it's likely that you'll hear this phrase a few thousand times during your trip down rock and roll's Yellow Brick Road. First off, most people who tell you, "You know, you should really be more like the winner of *American Idol*!" have no idea what "making it" means, if it means anything at all. The truth is, there are three trillion ways of making it. Making it means a different thing to everyone. To some, it's about getting to date Drew Barrymore, while to others, it's about winning a free pitcher of ale for singing "Mustang Sally" for a table of friends at your local hangout. Making it means everything, and it means nothing. Making it is an illusion, because there's no concrete definition about what it is. Most artists who've made it are actually more concerned with where their next great song is going to come from than whether or not they've made it. Remember: there are lots of unfulfilled superstars out there. For some of them, making it doesn't end up meaning what they thought it would. Colin Hay of Men At Work (whose debut album in the early 1980s yielded two number-one singles) once told a profound, if sad, anecdote about playing live on the Grammy Awards show, then being shuttled from stage to limousine, and from limousine to hotel. One minute, he was performing for millions of people worldwide; the next he was sitting on the edge of a hotel bed, wondering where the party was.

He'd made it.

There's no rock-and-roll blueprint. It's not like studying a manual and learning how to build a Battlebot. You can't diagram it and watch it come to life. The very proof of this lies in the galaxy of rock and roll's accidental stars, big names who never intended to have their voices heard outside the shower. Both Elvis and Dion (whose first big hit was "Runaround Sue") started out making records as presents for their mothers. In Elvis's case, the man who would go on to electroshock American culture was chronically insecure about his talents. It wasn't until he decided to reward his mother's faith in him by recording a song for her that he ever saw the inside of a studio (back in the 1950s, studios were the only means of recording, computers having not yet been invented). After the sessions – which cost him a grand sum of four dollars – the studio's manager, Sam Phillips, thought of Elvis when the time came to record a song he thought could be a hit. Phillips remembers having his secretary call the young singer about going over the song, "Without Love," and Elvis arrived before she even hung up the phone. Phillips asked Elvis how he'd traveled the distance (over a mile) so fast. Elvis told him that he ran.

Rod Stewart was discovered (by Long John Baldry) while singing to himself in a train station on the way to his job as a gravedigger. The world had never heard from blues legend Leadbelly until folklorist Alan Lomax recorded him as a fifty-year-old inmate doing time in a Louisiana prison, and the Bee Gees got their big break after being spotted by a promoter at a decrepit auto speedway in Brisbane, Australia. Even Frank Sinatra was discovered by happenstance, after bandleader Harry James heard him sing on a late-night radio broadcast. The following day, James drove out to the roadhouse that had hosted the broadcast, but was told by the manager that there was no vocalist. "We don't have a singer, I'm afraid," he said. "We only have a waiter who acts as an MC [master of ceremonies] and sings – a bit."

While there are hundreds of stars who fell backwards into fame, there are just as many musicians who, from the minute they jumped the cradle, were focused on making it. Consider Ottawa's Paul Anka. There's nothing accidental about Anka's success. As a teenager, the singer was so determined to be discovered that he entered a Campbell's Soup contest to win a trip to New York City, where he hoped to attract the attention of music producers. The contest demanded that the entrant collect a significant number of soup wrappers, so Anka secured a job in a supermarket where he gathered up all the excess wrappers. In his down time, he scoured dumpsters and garbage cans for discarded tins of soup. Anka won the contest, headed for New York, and, two summers later when he was sixteen years old, signed his first record deal with ABC-Paramount Records.

Some musicians were born into their careers, having made it from the moment they were forced into the world. Sly Stone did his first recording when he was four years old, with his family's band, the Stewart Four. Don and Phil Everly (who performed as the Everly Brothers) used to stop in at KMA radio in Shenandoah, Iowa, to appear on their family's radio show before they were shuffled off to primary school (Don even hosted his own Saturday morning program when he was seven). As an eleven-year-old boy, Gordon Lightfoot used to serenade the student body over the school public-address system. When Aretha Franklin was a child, famous vocalists Mahalia Jackson and Sam Cooke would join her family around the dinner table, while Michael Jackson played the bars, theaters, and concert halls of America long before he was old enough for high school.

Only select musicians may be obsessed, but the idea of making it is a truth by which the entire record industry exists. Making it, according to the popular myth of the business, is about selling millions of records, living on tour buses, entertaining groupies, and being pampered with lavish deli trays, fantastic light shows, critical praise, and money, money, money. Sure, money helps. Money won't love you, but it'll help float you through fallow times. And hotel rooms with 700 channels and terry-cloth robes and little pillow mints certainly trump hazardous flats over war-zone bars that the cops are too scared to visit, or floor-level flea-baggers where, as one musician told me, "there was no window, it was forty-below outside, and, in the morning, I awoke to find a snowbank at the end of my room." Tour buses do make the legs last longer – you can even catch a snooze if the road demands it – and elaborate "riders" specifying dressing-room cuisine afford rogue musicians the opportunity to snack in style when the schedule prevents them from properly eating lunch or dinner. Before the Rheostatics opened for the Tragically Hip at the brand new Corel Centre in Ottawa, sitting in our dressing room at a table laden with cheese, fruit, flatbread, twelve kinds of dip, expensive wine, and fresh flowers was like being in a restaurant that, outside of this rock-and-roll dream, I couldn't possibly afford.

But none of this means anything if the music isn't there. After a while, traveling on tour buses with the Rheos made me long for vans, because buses push you apart rather than pull you together. Similarly, I found as many reasons to dislike big hotels – Fourteen dollars for a video? What d'ya mean they can't press my suit until tomorrow morning? There's no club sandwich on the room-service menu? No gravy on the fries? – as I did ugly, cold motels. I was just as happy eating at King Falafel before playing Call

the Office in London, Ontario, as sampling French cuisine
backstage at the Bell Centre in Montreal. When we played
as openers for the Hip, the stage was so big that you could
have parked a Buick between us, which made me long for a
cramped bar with a postage-stamp stage and people
hanging from the ceiling. And no amount of luxury meant
anything if I blew out my voice, broke a string, lost my way
on a series of chord changes, fried my amp, forgot the
words during a critical part of the song, yelled at a
bandmate – or was yelled at – and felt like crap during,
before, or after a show. It makes no difference whether
you're heading back to the Four Seasons or the Four Jacks
after the show if your heart has betrayed you during a
performance. At the end of the night, you close your eyes
and everything is dark anyway.

I'm lucky to have played with the same core of musicians
for the last twenty-three years. I've made it in one sense.
Gord Downie once said of his band that the Tragically Hip
were the best because they'd been around the longest.
Some folks would say that the Rheostatics haven't made it,
and that's fine, which is exactly my point: everyone's idea
of making it is different. Where it gets muddled, however,
is when one person tries to impose their notion of making
it on another. And that, folks, is where the record company
comes in.

ROCK TALK
Getting Signed

Record companies are businesses of varying size and scope that *sign* artists to make records exclusively for them. The legal jargon is the domain of lawyers and accountants, but the way it works is usually this: record company employee (*A&R*, or Artists and Relations, scout) hears demo tape, likes demo tape, sees band perform, likes band live, offers band a contract to record under their *label*. *Demo tapes* are, generally, early recordings of a band's best songs. Sometimes the quality of the tape/CD matters, but often the A&R person is looking at the strength of song, the singing, and the playing. At music festivals and *conferences*, hundreds of bands are, more or less, competing to be heard – and liked and signed – by A&R reps of labels.

Not all record companies, of course. But signing with a record company, agreeing with it to put out your records under one of its labels, is a common indicator that you've made it, at least in the conventional sense. Before our first, crucial show in New York City in 1990 (as part of a popular music conference called the New Music Seminar),

I wandered around the Greenwich Village club, Kenny's Castaways, only to find the room full of record-company types with laminated name tags looped around their necks. I was gripped with anxiety and fear until I looked a little closer and realized that the companies they represented were outfits like Juggler Records, Acme Music, the Angry Noise Foundation. My point is that not every signing means going on the payroll at a big record company like Geffen or EMI. Sometimes it is no more significant than renewing your subscription to *National Geographic*. Besides, when I look back on that gig, I don't think about who was watching us as much as how we played. Because really, once you're in that moment – your body moving freely, your blood high, your mind floating as you create the art that you feel you are, in that instant, somehow born to make – it doesn't matter where you are, what you look like, what your image is, who's your stylist, what record company signed you, how much money they offered, how many soup labels you collected, or whether anyone's even listening, because, in the eyes of the rock-and-roll gods, you've made it. You're creating something as wild and beautiful as you were on the day the doctor held you upside down and you cried your first tear.

During that same trip, a friend of mine was signed to a major label. She asked me, years later, if I'd had a moment

similar to hers, when she stood at the window of the
Chelsea Hotel, looked out over the great city, and felt as if
she'd ascended to another realm – as if, finally, she'd made
it. I told her that, apart from our gig at Kenny's, I didn't
think so, even though we had traveled a similar route with
the same label: Sire.

For a solid year, the Rheostatics were wined and dined by
record company executives. I was reminded of when David
Geffen tried to woo Kurt Cobain into signing with his
label. Apparently, Geffen brought Cobain to a window in
his office overlooking a parking lot, where two Rolls
Royces sat next to each other. Geffen, allegedly, told
Cobain, "Sign with me, and you can drive away in one of
those." I'll admit that those kinds of encounters – though
none of mine, sadly, had anything to do with a Rolls Royce
– were thrilling the first few times they happened. But
after a while, hanging out with record company A&R types
was like visiting distant relatives to whom you're required
to be nice.

We'd sit in restaurants, bars, or fancy offices and listen to
their predictions of greatness, trying to read whether
they actually meant what they were saying. Once, we
were the guests of the Warner/Chappell publishing

empire on the thirtieth floor of a New York tower. It was
a catered affair in a sprawling committee room with the
finest nouvelle cuisine, and every few seconds, in would
walk a different employee who had something to do with
breaking our careers in the United States. I met the
original bass player for NRBQ, one of my favorite bands.
Martin Tielli, our guitarist, was talking to the head of the
company when Frank Sinatra's voice came over the
speaker phone. It was all pretty neat, apart from having
to hear our new record *Introducing Happiness* played
over and over, and feeling terribly self-conscious trying
to relate to these important strangers.

Upon leaving the building, I looked back and saw the
Cramps standing on the sidewalk. If you don't know, the
Cramps are one of the most respected and longstanding
American Punk bands. Their principals are a husband and
wife duo, Lux Interior and Poison Ivy, who were dressed,
as they are on most days, in leopard skin and leather. Out
on the street, they had a look of boredom and fatigue.
Beside them was a cart stacked with albums and CDs,
which they eventually loaded into the trunk of a cab.

As a twenty-year-old club kid, I had seen the Cramps play
at the Concert Hall on Yonge Street in Toronto. Lux stuffed

the microphone down his throat and sang like a demon.
Over the course of the evening, his pants sneaked down
until half his rump was showing. Four or five times, he fell
into the crowd, which passed him around the room on a
sea of hands. After the encore, Lux threw the microphone
to the floor, hiked up his drawers, and walked offstage to
roars of delight, bathing in the glory of having made it.

Now, here he was, catching a cab. We watched Lux and Ivy
load the records, ten at a time, into the trunk and back
seat, as we were whisked away to another record company
meeting. Seeing my heroes on the sidewalk reminded me
that, in one way, making it also means having to weather
the trials of life no differently than someone who works
down at the corner store, sells shoes at the mall, or cold
calls you at dinnertime to push opera subscriptions. Even
though they'd made twenty or so albums, toured the
world, and had scads of stories written about them, the
Cramps would soon be digging into their pockets for the
$7.50 needed to pay for the taxi, fumbling with their keys
once they got to their apartment, and retiring, sore-
legged, after they'd brought all of their records upstairs.
Perhaps, having carried in the last stack of discs, Lux
would turn to Ivy, wipe his brow, and tell her, "Whew. We
finally made it."

While all of this was going on, I'd be digging into my expensive arugula salad, at which point the record executive would lean over the table and promise that, in a few years, I'd never have to carry my own amp again.

A Very Slow Hand

Your First Instrument

While all of this talk of making it (or not making it) is enchanting, let's not get too far ahead of ourselves. Before you can even come close to recording hit albums, eating arugula salad, or hauling records up three flights of stairs to your Manhattan loft, you must have a conduit for your musical expression: which is to say, an instrument. In my case, it's a guitar. Despite having dabbled in bass and the occasional bashing of the drums, I'm predisposed to the six-string. This means that the next few pages will be weighted with guitar anecdotes, even though there's as much lore concerning the bass, keyboards, and, especially, the drum kit. Still, as a guitarist, I wouldn't want a synthesizer player telling me what to do with my SG, so I'll avoid those myths and legends out of respect for the other players' poison.

Whatever's hanging over your shoulder, buying your first instrument is always a big deal. Buying your first *real* instrument is even bigger, since teenage rockists almost always start with a discount version or copy of a popular brand. This is partly the result of parental trepidation. Most moms and dads of budding Satrianis are loathe to spend hundreds of dollars on a Fender Stratocaster, Gibson Les Paul, Taylor, or Larrivée guitar (or Fender P or MusicMan bass), only to have it prop open a closet door, or to see it transformed into a glorified tie-rack. This is where the copies come in and, while they almost always fall short of the brand they're aping, a Ledo, Samick, or El Degas has an awkward charm all its own, and looks no less real when squinted at from the back of a club.

Parents of rock-and-roll children aren't wrong in suggesting that young musicians acquire their arsenal from the ground up. Some of the world's most gifted guitarists have taken this notion to the extreme, building their first instruments rather than picking them out of a showroom. Brian May of Queen carved his famous Red Special with his father, using a piece of mahogany – plucked from a friend's garbage pile, no less – for the neck, and a slab of an old oak mantelpiece for the body. The guitar cost $50 (not counting the traditional sixpence that May uses as a guitar pick) and he has played it his entire career.

Industriousness, it seems, is an important part of early rock-and-roll life. Les Paul (for whom the famous guitar is named) transformed modern music after designing an electric guitar out of an old acoustic one, plugging the body with socks, shorts, towels, and even bits of plaster to give it a more raucous tone. Les remembers that the weight of his new creation made playing live impossible, so he built a new instrument using a four-by-four block of wood. The Log became rock's first electric guitar. Another guitar giant, Chet Atkins, used whatever was at hand to keep playing. Whenever he broke a string off his first guitar (it was actually a ukulele), he'd rip a wire off the screen door and thread it over the neck. Angus Young of AC/DC was even more industrious. Whenever he broke a finger – which he did many times, falling off amps or stage risers – he'd use the splints to play slide guitar.

As a teenager, Black Sabbath's Tommy Iommi was working at a factory when he caught the middle and ring fingers of his fretting hand in a metal press, one day before he was to leave on his first rock-and-roll tour in Germany. The doctor, seeing that the tips of both fingers had been

severed, told the guitarist that he'd never play again.
Unbowed, Iommi melted down a bottle of Fairy Liquid
(dishwashing detergent) and fashioned thimbles to keep
his fingers from being ripped open by the strings. Because
he relied on his two good fingers to play – the thimbles
had the tendency to slip – Iommi accidentally invented the
power chord, laying a single finger over the bottom five
strings. Still, it wasn't until the manager of the factory
turned him on to Django Reinhardt, the great Gypsy jazz
guitarist who was half-paralyzed in one hand, that he
found the inspiration to become one of the great rock
guitarists of his time.

In a way, every kid has a handicap when it comes to
learning how to rock. Not to belittle Iommi's
achievements, but those first few months scrubbing a
guitar are murder on anyone's digits, at least until the
calluses set in (Atkins remembers laying a kitchen knife
across the strings whenever his fingers felt too tender to
play). I toughened my skin as a thirteen-year-old at a place
called Ken Jones Music at the Westway Plaza (our
neighborhood strip mall), which is also where I bought my
first guitar.

Ken's shop was located at the back of the plaza.
Developers, I think, had put it there so that its greasy-

haired, bell-bottomed patrons and employees would be
out of view from the rest of the suburban shoppers. While
its lone, dirt-smudged window stared out at a parking lot,
which bordered a sagging gray apartment complex, the
store itself was a bubbling planet of life, crowded with the
kind of freaks I'd only ever seen in the pages of rock
magazines. Young men and women (being pre-Courtney
Love, pre-Lilith Fair, and pre-Spice and Riot Grrrl
movements, it was mostly men) wearing beaded denim
jackets, platform shoes, and coats with fake fur on the
collars sat atop amps, playing popular riffs and runs on
their custom axes. On busy weekend afternoons, these
Lions of the Fuzztone commingled with awkward, tight-
faced kids like myself who passed through Ken's looking
glass in search of musical enlightenment.

Ken Jones, the store's proprietor, was a beatific, slouch-
shouldered man with a trustful way who gave lessons in a
tiny crawlspace that ran off the side of the showroom.
Actually, "showroom" is too impressive a word to describe
the store. The area where the guitars, basses, banjos, and a
single mandolin hung was probably no bigger than your
dad's tool shed. It was a close room, often consumed by a
cloud of tobacco smoke. As a result, I felt like I was in a
forest of music, the great bodies of Hohners and Birdlands

ROCK TALK
Guitarspeak

One of the fun things about the language of rock and roll is that there's a whole rockspeak that's evolved over the years. A *riff*, for instance, is a repeated figure, or run, or *lick*, that appears several times throughout a song (a *hook* is like this, too), hence the terms "riffman" or "riffmeister" or "riff rock." *Slide guitar* is a style of playing using a bottleneck or similarly shaped device to play over the fretboard, instead of using one's fingers (blues and country-blues are the progenitors of slide playing). A guitar is often called an *axe*, thus a male guitarist might be an "axeman." Drummers are called many things, but here I've called them "trappists" and "trapsmen" ("traps" being a vaudevillian term for tom toms), and a *drum fill* is anything that isn't a simple beat. A *middle-eight* is traditionally the part of the song that isn't a verse or chorus – and, yup, comes in the middle and has eight bars. It is often the domain of American bands, as it has been noted that the British will more often repeat the chorus than pause for a melodic break.

and Gibson 335s waving overhead, their glinting tuning
pegs, machine heads, chrome pick guards, and gold
volume knobs shining like fireflies through the trees.

While waiting to take a lesson with Ken, I'd sit against a
wall racked with songbooks of bands whose names – ZZ
Top, Van der Graaf Generator, the Moody Blues – sounded
like comic book characters I hadn't yet discovered. Ken –
who wore a perpetual brown suit and vest – suggested I
start with Mel Bay's *How to Play Guitar* book, which I
drew from between *The Best of Carol King* and Led
Zeppelin's *Houses of the Holy*. Because I was using a
rented, nylon-string Spanish guitar, I was shepherded
through a mild repertoire of "Michael, Row the Boat
Ashore" and "Kumbaya," which, as you can imagine, was
disappointing to a kid eager to find out how Jimmy Page
made his guitar sound like a creaking cellar door on "D'yer
Mak'er." After requesting a change in direction from Ken, I
was passed on to a 1970s riff-rock star capable of spinning
long, twenty-minute guitar odysseys, his tongue curved
over his top lip, hair slung across his eyes, corduroy-kneed
legs angled together in rock-and-roll ecstasy.

I realize that the blessed few among you whose foreheads
were tapped by Paganini's bow after being freed from your
mother's womb might feel compelled to feed this book to

your hamster after reading my next confession, but unless
you can drum Frank Zappa's "The Black Page," or fret Van
Halen's "Eruption," or play the bass solo in Yes's
"Roundabout," please hang with me while I tell you that,
in my early days of learning rock guitar, the experience
was as much fun and as rewarding as dental surgery. In the
beginning, I had a terrible time trying to play rock guitar –
especially soloing. Whenever I played "Stairway to Heaven,"
the notes sounded the way letters look after being emptied
from a Scrabble bag. They were incomprehensible.
Eventually, I was downgraded from trying the solo, to
copping the middle-eight chords, to learning the light,
plucking intro. When that failed, I spent my lesson with
my guitar laid across my lap while the instructor wailed on
the seat across from mine, his fingers crawling over his
guitar neck like baby snakes being born.

But then, two things happened. First, my parents bought
me an electric guitar: a white, Stratocaster-copy El Degas
with black tone knobs. It was exactly like the guitar on the
cover of Eric Clapton's *Slowhand*, an image I copied while
standing in front of our mirrored hallway pretending to be
a blues/rock potentate wooing the masses. While my new
axe possessed a neck with about as much give as a church
pew, it was mine. I was free to imbue it with my own
sweat and spit and strain, with whatever music I could

play. I hacked and slashed at the pick guard without worrying about leaving unwanted rock-and-roll graffiti, bending and twisting and wrenching its neck to match the awkwardness of my own hands and fingers. The sound might have been bad, the notes wrong.

But, for the first time, it was *Dave*.

The other thing that happened was that I discovered music – and musicians – beyond the songbooks on Ken's wall. I'm grateful to Punk and New Wave music for showing me that rock-and-roll virtuosity goes beyond impossibly fast guitar runs or progressive epics with neo-classical references that fill up an entire side of a record. One of the reasons I'd been so discouraged in my guitar playing was because folks like Alex Lifeson, Frank Marino, Joe Walsh, and Ritchie Blackmore had set the bar so impossibly high. I soon discovered that playing like Cheetah Chrome of the Dead Boys was no problem at all. Other bands, like the Ramones, the Clash, and Sex Pistols, proved that rock and roll wasn't only about dazzling music shop trolls with one's manual dexterity or knowing what a pentatonic scale is. It meant playing from your heart and with enthusiasm, which I had in spades. Johnny Ramone, for his part, said, "Just being yourself is intelligent." So I decided to be myself. One year later, the Rheostatics were formed.

Soon, I met other kids – including my friend and bandmate Tim Vesely, who played bass – who were into the same thing. Once you love a band, or a scene, sound, movement, or genre, you wear it like a tall, flowery hat, announcing it to the rest of the world. Like a streetlight to a burst of bugs, one's allegiance to a certain kind of music attracts like-minded kids. I'm often asked what's the best way for a young musician to find the right people to play with, and while I have no smart answer, it's no coincidence that thousands of bands have been formed out of small groups of people worshipping the same music. Like any relationship, it helps when folks share the same interests or passion. One of the great things about those early Rheos gigs was discovering hundreds of kids who were into the same bands as we were. At our third gig at a downtown Toronto rock club – the Edge, circa 1980 – I looked into the crowd and saw kids who dressed, talked, and danced like us, but who came from places three, four districts away, on the other side of the tracks. Once this connection was made, we bonded, and grew tough against the world. Knowing you're not alone is critical. You think, *If others can do it, I can do it, too.*

Once I fell into my own scene (in the early days of Toronto New Wave, it was actually too small to be considered a movement or trend) I noticed that most of the other

bands used crappy equipment, too. Still, the music
sparkled. I remember seeing the British band Gang of Four
play at an old dancehall by the lake. They had even worse
instruments than my own – cheap British knock-offs of
American brands – but the gig was fantastic. The group's
lead singer, Jon King, jumped so high that he smashed his
head on a pipe above the stage, knocking himself
unconscious. Drummer Hugo Burnham came out from
behind the kit and sang, the first time I'd ever seen a
drummer do anything other than just drum. King was
revived and the set continued. The band had shown heart,
resolve, determination. It was really something.

One of the cool things about Kurt Cobain is that he played
a Fender Mustang, a guitar that's considered among the
lesser Fenders, more affordable than a high-end Strat or
Telecaster. That his band would eventually rule the world
of popular music says something about the importance of
how you play, rather than what you play. Ornette
Coleman, one of the great modern jazz pioneers, forged
his reputation on a toy saxophone. Ricky Wilson of the
B-52's played his entire career with just three strings.
Willie Nelson's guitar has a big hole in it.

In 1957, Buddy Knox set out to record the song "Party
Doll" with the sole purpose of making a handful of

records as keepsakes for friends and bandmates. With $60 in his pocket, he booked time at Norman Petty's studio in Clovis, New Mexico, which would become home to many of Buddy Holly's most famous recordings. When they started to make sounds, both Knox and his bass player, Jimmy Bowen, realized that Bowen couldn't play. So Petty hired a local musician for the session, and suggested as well that the drummer in Petty's trio, Dave Alldred, sit in on the gig. But since Alldred didn't have a complete drum kit, Petty and company improvised. They filled a cardboard box with cotton and stuffed a microphone deep inside, and a couple of girls from the Clovis High School marching band were recruited to play cymbals. Everyone took home a demo of the song to play it to friends. One day, local radio disk jockey Dean Kelly accidentally put it on the air. A few months later, "Party Doll" was the number-one record in the U.S.

These musicians created rock-and-roll magic despite the value – or lack of value – of what they carried in their hands. This is not to disparage the beauty of a '53 Broadcaster guitar or a vintage Gretsch drum kit, but the player makes the instrument, not the other way around. In my life, I've only ever owned three electric guitars. Sure, I've desired the mythic five-necked Hamer played by Cheap Trick's Rick Nielsen, but every time I plug in my smudge-black Gibson Howard Roberts – a guitar named after a jazz guitarist few people have ever heard of – it sounds the way I do. Which is joyful, angry, sad, weary, or euphoric. That's the most any artist can want from his instrument.

Playing in a Travelin' Band

Getting Along in Spite of It All

The Chambers Brothers were a San Francisco psychedelic soul band – forerunners of a short-lived 1960s movement, it turned out – who moved, en masse, out of their parents' homes to live in one big house. In the beginning, they were poor. They gigged and gigged and were lost in the wilderness until a song called "Time Has Come Today" put them on the pop/rock map. But before then, they subsisted almost exclusively on peanuts. They'd buy an enormous bottle of pop, drain the soda, collect the deposit, and buy three-foot-high bags of nuts. It wasn't what anyone would call a nutritious diet, but it kept them in the game long enough to get their hit record, which is all that matters when you're trying to rise above the pack.

Chances are, every band you've ever cared about has
suffered at the beginning, though it never really feels like
suffering when it's happening, since it's so new and
different and exotic. This is especially true for kids who,
after being harbored by their parents for most of their lives,
are thrilled to be living along the rough-hewn edges of life.
I'm not trying to glamorize penury, but there's something
about a band having to split $20 four ways – which the
Rheos did after earning a pittance for an out-of-town gig
opening for John Otway – that draws musicians together.

It's not uncommon for the rehearsal space to become the
de facto home of teenage rock-and-roll runaways. After
awhile, you spend so much time there that you end up
crashing behind the drum kit, using a soft guitar case as
your pillow. This is despite the fact that jam spaces are
generally some of the most decrepit buildings I've ever
been in, run by the weirdest creeps at the lowest end of the
music racket. The rooms – and occasionally the creeps –
smell like urine and vomit. They're often in the worst parts
of town because, like half-way houses or rehab centers, no
decent neighborhood would ever allow a place solely
patronized by musicians to be raised in its midst. Like
punk, dance, and gay clubs, rehearsal spaces take root in the
industrial ends of town where buildings on their last legs
can be occupied for cheap rent. There's hardly ever enough

heat in the wintertime, the security is negligible, and power ebbs and flows (in one otherwise forgettable space, our sound system died every time the neighbor revved his skillsaw). We've had our equipment stolen only once from a rehearsal space – a favorable statistic, for which I'm grateful to the rock-and-roll gods – but the thieves made off with irreplaceable vintage basses and guitars, which were never recovered. In the best instances, jam factories are beehives of activity where you're able to cross paths with bands on the way up and down – trading club contacts, sharing gear, hanging out, talking shop. In the worst cases, your room is sandwiched between hideously loud cover bands playing dueling versions of Steppenwolf's "Magic Carpet Ride." But in the early days, you rarely have a choice. You play the cards that are dealt to you.

Our first rehearsal space was the nicest. It was in Rod Westlake's parents' house, in a nice part of town, no less. Rod was our original drummer. The year I turned fifteen, the band was Tim Vesely on bass, Rod on drums, a fellow named Dave Crosby on keyboards, and me on guitar (for the record, Dave Clark replaced noted jazz trappist Graham Kirkland, who briefly replaced Rod; Martin Tielli, on guitar and vocals, came a few years later). We rehearsed three times a week in the Westlakes' basement, which was hung with Rod's mom's macrame wall hangings and his brother's Pink Floyd posters. Rod was a hyperactive kid who played on a drum riser that had been built so we could simulate a "concert setting" in the basement. His skittishness was such that he often appeared to be vibrating like a sprung doorstop even when standing still. This mad energy, however, complemented his speedy drumming and the fact that, as a band, we couldn't learn how to rock fast enough.

Crosby played a synthesizer with knobs imprinted with sine waves. He was a stiff-legged beanpole whose hair framed his high forehead in perfect half-moons. Together, we wrote songs like "The People Who Live on Plastic Lake" and "Sometimes I Feel Like An Elevator" – New Wave, sci-fi slabs that featured plucky bass lines and whooping synthesizer patterns. I'd stand behind most of those early numbers if it weren't for something called "A Letter to the President," a haunting knuckle-biter that included a section read by yours truly in a British accent. My friends often remind me that I used to speak this way, not just when singing, but also in normal conversation. It seems that, for three or four years, every time I opened my mouth, I sounded like Austin Powers. It's a wonder no one ever slapped me on the head and told me to stop talking like an idiot.

Our first demo tape included four songs: "On TV,"
"Suburb Shuffle," "Radio 80 Fantasy," and "Letter to the
President." One of the people I sent the tape to was Gary
Topp, who was talent booker for a club called the Edge.
Since we didn't hear anything for weeks, I figured that our
music had fallen on deaf ears. But one afternoon, I found
myself at the New Yorker Theatre on Yonge Street, where
I'd been sent to review *The Great Rock and Roll Swindle* for
a high-school newspaper. Gary Topp was there, too. As it
turned out, he'd called my home that day and told my
mom that he could give us an opening spot on a
weeknight. When I first spotted him at the theater, I tried
not to stare; he was one of the most influential New Wave
concert promoters in Canada.

I was flabbergasted when he walked over and said, "Excuse
me, are you Dave?" I told him that I was, and he told me
that he really liked our tape. I couldn't believe it. I phoned
my mom and then I phoned Tim, who called the rest of
the guys. We had our first gig.

This is from my first book, *On A Cold Road*:

> When we played the Edge, I had no idea what I was
> supposed to do. Let me correct that. I had too many

ideas. I'd imagined myself a thousand different ways,
visualizing moves, cues, lyrics, guitar parts, stage
clothes, between-song banter, the set list, everything.
For weeks, I'd dreamed the performance over and
over in my head, but once on stage, I ended up being
myself. And it was okay. I think we played ten songs.
Our friends came in packs and sat in the front; our
parents came together and sat at the back. There were
many thrilling firsts. Being in a dressing room.
Setting up our equipment. Watching the other band
arrive (I remember one of them arrived in a cab,
which struck me as wildly eccentric). Getting a free
Coke at the bar. Taking a piss in the stall with stickers
and graffiti everywhere. Seeing our name on the flyer
alongside XTC and Split Enz and the Demics. Talking
to the waitresses. Looking into the upstairs office and
seeing the promoter's desk stacked with papers.
Sitting at a table under a window in the falling
evening light, writing out our set list as the
soundman unwrapped microphone cables and
organized the stage. Cigarette burns and gum on the
carpet. The stink of grease. The reek of beer. The way
the traffic slowed outside and the streets emptied
until suddenly a handful of people walked around the
corner talking to each other, then climbed the few
steps of the club, passed through the big wooden

doors, and paid the tired-looking woman who sat at the table near the entrance. These were people we didn't know. Adults. Were they here to see us?

Rod played one live gig with us, Crosby several more. Both eventually left the band, the first in a parade of ex-members that includes Seth the Magician, a fat, goateed prestidigitator who nearly tricked us into being his back-up band by promising us a regular gig at a restaurant called Ginsberg and Wong; Blue Rodeo's current keyboardist James Grey, who drank a shocking amount of strong coffee and brought us something that we just couldn't grasp at the time – actual talent; and the Trans Canada Soul Patrol Horns, a trio of pros who quit the group to support Brenda Lee and other country and soul superstars at a converted K-Mart store famous for having the world's longest bar, which saxophonist Dave Rodenberg hoped would help him realize his goal of a steady musician's income and the hair replacement procedure he'd dreamed about since high school.

Looking back, both Rod's and Dave's departures from the band were more difficult than they should have been. But we were groping in the dark when it came to people skills. Rod's departure was entirely my fault. In the Westlakes' basement, his brother had stashed a collection of stolen

Stop signs and other traffic-related paraphernalia. One day, as an after-school joke, I pretended to phone the cops to report stolen property. I hadn't quite hung up the phone before shooting my mouth off, so the operator at the other end (I had dialed O to lend the prank a touch of reality) traced the call, then immediately telephoned the cops. Later that day, after baseball practice, I found my amplifier sitting in my room. It had been delivered to my house by Rod's dad, who'd banned me from ever setting foot on his property after being visited during dinner by the local police, armed with a writ to search the Westlake household.

Dave Crosby's exodus was sadder still. I blame myself for casting out one of my best friends, and, until that point, the funniest person I'd ever met. The beginning of the end came in Dave Clark's parents' cozy, wood-paneled basement, where we rehearsed for the better part of a decade. Crosby had a habit of getting to practice before us so that he could play the odd prank and crack us up. Sometimes he'd scare us by leaping out of a closet or back room where he'd been hiding. One day after school, Tim, Dave Clark, and I went back to the Clarks' to talk about letting Crosby go from the band. I can't remember why we decided to axe him; maybe it was that the jokes were getting stale, or maybe it was one of those stupid things where losing friends is just a symptom of the passing of time. Since Dave had been making overtures about wanting to play in the NBA, and because he wasn't into rehearsing as much as we were, the notion of firing him was unanimous. It was just a case of figuring out how to administer the news. After a few minutes, we adjourned to the upstairs kitchen, where Mrs. Clark was sitting.

"When are you boys going to start playing?" she asked.

"We're not. Crosby's not here," we said.

"Yes, he is. He arrived about fifteen minutes ago."

We looked at each other.

We went back downstairs.

Dave was sitting on the couch watching television.

He turned around.

"Hey, guys!" he said, waving.

It's a wonder that we never came to blows, but, as it turned out, there was plenty of time for that. The relationships in the Rheostatics have been so tight over the years that, like any set of brothers or sisters, the threat of physical violence (and outright war and jealousy) has occasionally come between us. Those early days of poverty and close quarters and raw-nerved artistic expression often exacerbated whatever tension – good or bad – we were feeling as individuals or a collective.

Rock bands have a history of beating the snot out of each other, so, should you find yourself either giving or receiving the blunt end of a knuckle sandwich, you're merely part of a continuum that is one of the classic conditions of rock and roll. The Kinks, for instance, were notorious brawlers. A friend of mine was riding in a cab with Peter Quaife, the ex-Kink bassist, who revealed how he'd decided to quit the band after Ray Davies broke his jaw a second time. Pete Townshend and Roger Daltrey of the Who used to get into it all the time. Townshend had roadies hold down Daltrey while the guitarist filled his gut with body blows. Drummer Keith Moon was the most benevolent of the three, but this didn't stop him from hiring a convicted murderer as his security shepherd. Graham Chapman, the late Monty Python actor and writer, once told me that Moon's thug used to carry a kitchen knife with him at all times. Once, at one of Moon's parties, the thug grew suspicious of one of the guests, and within seconds had him pinned to the floor with the blade dangling above the partygoer's throat. Reacting smartly (Moon was nowhere to be found), Chapman strode up to the goon and suggested that Moon wouldn't be pleased to find bloodstains on his new, white shag carpet. The reveler was freed and a life was spared.

When the Rolling Stones were on tour in the 1970s, Mick Jagger returned near morning to rouse the rest of the band from sleep so that he'd have someone to keep partying with. He stormed into the room where Charlie Watts was sleeping and announced, "I want my drummer dressed and downstairs in five minutes!"

Charlie stirred himself from slumber, showered, put on his finest suit, slicked back his hair, and went down into the lobby where Mick was waiting. He walked up to Jagger and laid him out with one punch. Standing over him, he said, "I'm not going out and I'm not *your* drummer. You're *my* singer." He returned to his room, got into his pajamas and went back to sleep.

The only time it got really bad with the Rheos was while we were on tour in Ireland in 1988. Having no money, playing crummy shows, and living in a youth hostel didn't exactly make for a state of frolicking joy and love. Touring Ireland had been an outright gamble in the first place.

Even though we had no album, video, or hit single – or record company, for that matter – to support us, we remained stubborn in our dream (okay, my dream; at twenty-two, I'd studied at Trinity College, Dublin, and had had the time of my life) to tour the Emerald Isle.

During an earlier trip to Dublin, I'd met a girl named Edwina, who ended up being our Irish agent.

"So, you really think you can get us gigs?" I asked upon meeting her.

"Oh, ya. Brilliant," she said.

"Good gigs?" I asked.

"Brilliant!" she replied.

"Gigs for money?"

"Oh, ya, the money would be brilliant."

"Brilliant, eh?"

"Oh, ya, brilliant!"

I told Martin, Tim, and Dave that a tour of Ireland would be brilliant. Everyone agreed that you couldn't get much better than that. So we said, "Okay, let's go," telling Edwina to book it and we would come.

"Brilliant" was one of those words that I heard over and over again, in the pubs, hostels, cafes, and clubs that we frequented during our stay. Another expression was, "Are you going to see the Horde?" I didn't understand either of them.

Our first show was at the Ball in Trinity College, a concert for first-year university students in one of the world's most famous schools. I must say that the only brilliant thing about it was the vomit. I've never seen more puke in my entire life. Kids were skating and swimming in it, chin down in it, fashioning robes and gloves and hats with it. In fact, they were so busy playing with their own bile that they hardly noticed us. After our set, a kid came up to me and told me that he thought that our music was brilliant.

"Oh, gee, thanks," I said.

"You're from Canada, then?" he asked.

I told him that we were.

"Listen, are you going to see the Horde?" he asked. "They're brilliant."

Our next show was in Cork. We loaded our equipment on the train and headed to the coast. We found ourselves in a car packed with small men in furry hats. They were hurling fans (hurling being a traditional Irish sport) traveling to an away match. "Play us a song, boys!" they screamed after seeing us carry our guitars on board.

"We're actually kinda tired," we told them.

"Nonsense," said one of the men. "What do you need – food?" he asked, producing a hunk of cheese the size of a radial tire and a handful of fruit, which he served to us in the cradle of his hurling cap.

"Um, we're not really hungry," we said.

"What do you need – drink?" he asked, pulling out a jug of clear whiskey – a concoction known as poteen – which he poured into little plastic cups. He did everything short of grabbing the back of our heads to get us to drink.

"Um, we're not really thirsty," we told him.

"LETS HEAR IT NOW!" he commanded, slapping the flat of his hand on his knee.

We had no choice. We gave him Stompin' Tom. We played for hours, fueled by the bizarre white liquid. After a while, we found ourselves wearing furry hats. The Irish countryside peeled past us and I realized where train songs come from.

In Cork, we played at a club with an enormous plastic spider web hanging over the dance floor. There were no lights onstage. The DJ was dressed like Dracula. He wore black and white face makeup, dragged around a withered cape, and smoked a cigarette. He announced us: "And now, ladies and gentlemen, all the way from Canada, er . . . er . . ."

And that was as far as he got. We started playing. About eighty kids approached the stage and stood there with their arms crossed. After ten songs, they hadn't moved. Alas, we finished and the DJ struck up the canned music, at which point the crowd began wildly gyrating. We packed up our gear and met two young girls who asked if we needed a place to stay. We did.

We went back to their tiny, two-room apartment and talked music. "Are you going to see the Horde?" they asked.

The four of us Rheos ended up sharing one bed. I awoke in the middle of the night to find one of my bandmates spearing me in the back of the head with his elbow as he flailed away, scratching the bottom of his feet. It was now, officially, a tour: Martin had athlete's foot.

The next gig was in Limerick. Limerick is the joyride capital of Ireland and it was the low point of the trip. We traveled there by train, slugging our gear – drums, guitars, cables – across the platform only to end up in a Texas-themed tavern called the Barn. In the land of great Irish poetry, we found posters of Tony Dorsett and the Dallas Cowboy Cheerleaders. When we got to the club, we also discovered that the promoters – whom we'd never met – had neglected to hire amplifiers for our guitars. Guitar and bass amps are called "backline" in Europe; we didn't know that word, so we could not request them. We ended up playing with our guitars plugged into a P.A. system, which lent our music the warmth of a chisel grinding stone.

By now, the brilliance had worn off the tour. Limerick should have been our worst show ever. But as the show

started, Dave Clark peeled off his shirt and wrapped
himself in the Canadian flag. He swung from a pipe across
the ceiling, like a professional wrestler. The show caught
fire and we had a great gig.

The rest of the trip, however, was a wild series of highs and
lows. Martin forgot his wallet at the bed and breakfast we
had stayed at. We convinced him to go back and retrieve it,
and he found the host family waiting for him in the
doorway, dressed in their Sunday best. Thinking it would
be rude to count the money in front of them, Martin
found on the train that 100 Irish pounds were missing. It
was all cheese sandwiches and half-pints of beer and
borrowed cigarettes for him the rest of the trip. But that
was pretty much his diet anyway.

Back in Dublin, we opened for the Jazz Butcher in the
Buttery, Trinity College's cafeteria. Once again, Dave Clark
appeared undressed from the waist up. We played three
songs before he jumped up from behind his kit, pointed a
drum stick at Martin, and started screaming at him. Then
he fled into the night. I kicked over a microphone stand
and went looking for my friend. I found him outside,
sitting at the base of a statue.

"We better go in and play," I offered.

"This tour is terrible," he said.

He was right. I blamed myself.

It all came to a head one afternoon at University College,
Dublin, where we waited to hear about a lunchtime
performance. But we never got the chance to play: the gig
was canceled because there was a student debate on
abortion. We sat on our amps feeling deflated and, for some
reason, started fighting about Neil Young.

Dave Clark and Martin were already into it when I joined
in, opening my mouth when I should have kept it shut.
One of us called Neil a "wanker" and Martin lost it. Before
I knew it, Martin had his hands around my throat. He
went bug-eyed and turned beet red – thinking back,
probably so did I – squeezing my neck. I tried to get free,
but he just squeezed harder. Just as I started to panic, he let
go and broke down in tears. I looked over my shoulder,
and Dave was running away again, this time with his shirt
on. I didn't go after him.

Our last show was at a nurses' college in Dundrum. We
showed up to discover that we'd be playing in a small
classroom. It was filled with eighteen-year-old girls passing

around a silver tea set and a plate of biscuits. Not only was there no backline or amp, there was no sound system at all. We shared the bill with a traditional Irish group, Kali, who lent us their acoustic guitars and bodhran (a small, hand-held drum). Before the show, one of the nursing students led me down a long dark hallway into a change room and opened up a cabinet, revealing the twenty-four cans of Budweiser she'd smuggled into the college. We drank them all at once. The gig was unmemorable, not because it was bad, but because I can remember none of it.

The show ended late, after the buses to Dublin had stopped running. The same student who'd supplied us with beer told us to bring our equipment to the curb, where she would hail us a ride into town. We were drunk. We were tired. We stank. We hated each other. A minibus pulled up and the young woman gestured for us to get on. We thanked her and proceeded to climb aboard. The bus was half-empty. It was dark and gloomy, yet it smelled like a garden. As I walked down the middle, I realized that I was surrounded by Irish beauties. As it turned out, the bus was carrying fifteen of the country's highest-paid fashion models, returning from a show up north. I sat beside one of them, and she leaned away, as if some unknown force was pulling her by her hair.

"Hello," I offered, smiling through my twenty-day beard and roadstink fog.

"Uh, hello," she said, turning her head.

Then I said the only thing I could think of.

"Are you going to see the Horde?"

The Squarest People in the World

Dressing for Success

Until I started playing rock and roll with the Rheostatics, I hated having to get dressed up. My parents used to force me into stiff-legged dress pants or shirts with hardened collars, pinned at the cuffs and clavicle. I would've had more freedom of movement had they draped me in chain mail and thrown me on a horse. But for the occasion of the Rheostatics' first few gigs, something compelled me to abandon my uniform of jeans, T-shirt, and running shoes in favor of suit jackets and nice trousers. Weirder still, I voluntarily went shopping for the first time in my life.

There are two schools of thought when it comes to dressing for the stage: to look as unassuming and as unlike you're on display as possible, or to dress with more boldness and flash than is recommended by governing authorities. Ideally, I think you want a little bit of both. Someone like Frank Sinatra or Brian Ferry, while they favored fine suits and tuxedoes, never appeared as if bound by their attire, mostly because the looseness of their musical styles contrasted with the formal nature of their clothes. Similarly, even though the guys in the Strokes dress like they're on their way to the laundromat, when the stage lights flicker and hiccup you suddenly notice the way a certain sleeve hangs or jeans bundle at the knee, as if purposefully so. Me, I've worn suits on stage ever since the early days, more for the appeal of their loose fit than anything. Not to sound too much like your mom here, but unless you've already made the conscious decision to carry the weight of an Elton John head plume or Marilyn Manson skin-sucking one-piece, it's best to give all your pores space to breathe. There's nothing worse than ending up boiled in your own sweat after a two-hour gig. Then again, there's also nothing better; though personally I find windmilling, stage-jumping, and riser-hopping much easier to do when your clothes are riding over your skin rather than hugging it.

This is not to suggest that comfort is the only standard by which musicians should outfit themselves. In the early

1990s, SoCal Punk spawned a fashion statement that
became, in many circles, a siren for the brainless: SOS
(Shorts On Stage). In the hot climate of Southern
California, it made sense that California Punks would
dress lightly so that they might rock to the best of their
abilities, but after a while, northern, western, and eastern
bands adopted the uniform, despite the hardier nature of
their indigenous climates. For a time, SOS was a scourge
on the land, fashion-wise. It was as if musicians had
collectively forgotten that one's knees are among the least
beautiful parts of one's body, and that flashing them in
public – unless you're Halle Berry or Australian swimmer
Ian Thorpe – is to take away from rock's visual experience
rather than to add to it. SOS is a signifier that the shorts-
wearer is strangely proud of his knees, which implies that
he might be into Hulk Hogan and the films of Bruce Willis
as well. In a side note, SoCal also gave us the rock-and-roll
goatee, a facial design that mirrored the greater public's
look, rather than confronted it. Not to overstate the
relationship between fashion and rock, but is it
coincidence that many of those goatee-wearing SOS bands
rang a little hollow when knocked, too?

On the Rheos' first Canadian tour in the summer of 1987,
we wore matching jackets of Canadian tartan: a red and
green serge designed to commemorate our country's

Centennial in 1967. We affected this look not only because
of our emerging interest in – and infatuation with –
Canada, but also because, one night in Peterborough, local
musician Washboard Hank gave us his. It seemed only
proper to follow the tartan trail, so we spent the next few
years scouring used-clothing shops for matching jackets.

I believe that used-clothing shops exist solely to outfit up-
and-coming bands. The entire Pacific Northwest Grunge
scene of the 1990s, it seems, was clothed from Sally Anns
and Variety Villages. This is a tradition that, I believe,
started with the mid-1980s New Wave band the B-52's, who
used to overturn junk shops for clothes, old keyboards,
electronics, and other stuff. It wasn't uncommon for them
to return home from shows with a couch strapped to their
van. Secondhand stores are perfect when you're trying to
get a look together for your band. The clothes are cheap
and occasionally you'll stumble across a pop artifact: the
purple golf visor, leather platform shoe, or green velour
sweater that'll make you the envy of your hip corner, if
you're concerned with such matters. Secondhand stores are
also great places to find cat-clawed records and crack-cased
CDs for the price of a bag of chips.

While on tour with the Tragically Hip in 1996, we voted –
Tim was defeated 3 to 1 – to dress in matching, purple

satin blazers. Our idea was to walk into the arena dressed like a failed lounge band, only to belie our soft look with a fierce, head-punching sound. That, and we wanted to look fab. Tim's argument against matching suits, I think, was based on the notion that, ever since the Beatles broke up, bands were no longer required to wear uniforms. He thought it was our duty to dress freely, since, unlike in the 1950s, society no longer demanded that we look like glee-club dropouts.

Rock's early uniforms were descendants of the big-band era, when club owners, promoters, and unions insisted that a musician dress formally for a gig. The Beatles' conceit was that, despite their nice threads and Nehru collars, they had hair that grew below their ears (!), suggesting a freedom of spirit beneath their otherwise conservative suits. It wasn't until the album *Revolver* that they finally abandoned their conservative look for paisley shirts and sandals. Ultimately, they lost all sense of propriety, dressing like grenadier guardsmen scribbled with neon markers for the cover of *Sergeant Pepper's Lonely Hearts Club Band.*

The Beatles' liberation from their matching suits caused the whole rock-and-roll fashion world to explode. Psychedelic bands turned up their noses at any fabric not

patterned with spacecraft or flowers; the denizens of Acid
Rock dressed in capes with long, fringed wings and wore
platform boots higher than Mini Me's belt loops; Prairie
Rock saw the advent of Trapper Chic, which included an
array of pelts, coonskin caps, and mukluks. Mick Jagger
wore a white dress to eulogize Brian Jones in Hyde Park;
David Bowie, Alice Cooper, and even that ragamuffin Bob
Dylan took to painting their faces in concert; the Tubes
dressed in drag, Motorhead in leather; and Elton John, the
most flamboyant artist of his time, was festooned like a
rooster on steroids. AC/DC's Angus Young first dressed in
a gorilla suit, and then a Zorro outfit, before deciding on
his trademark schoolboy's outfit. After a while, you almost
wished the Beatles would put their suits back on, but they
broke up too soon for that to happen. In the years
following the band's demise, it seemed as if musicians had
forgotten how they were supposed to sound, and worried
instead about whether their sunglasses would be visible
from outer space.

Punk brought fashion back to Earth, and left it in a heap of
safety pins and garbage bags. Truth be told, this was more
a legacy of their fans than the groups who whipped them
into a frenzy, even though the Sex Pistols evolved as the
brainchild of Malcolm McLaren, who ran SEX, a fashion
boutique in London's West End. I checked in around Joe

Jackson-era New Wave, and since Joe – like the Mods, the
Numbers, Squeeze, and the Jam, among many others – was
besuited, I followed his lead, eventually pilfering clothes
from my father's closet to wear on stage. Joe's fashion
statement, I think, was about dressing like a clerk in an era
when stadium-rock bands like ELO, Journey, Triumph, and
Trooper were touring with enormous trunks filled with
shiny jumpsuits. It was the first kind of nerd chic – a look
that's still reflected in the science-kid glasses and geeky
pants favored by dance kids. Since, at eighteen, the
uncoolest thing possible was to wear what your parents
wore, I had a great reservoir at my disposal. Which brings
me to another piece of advice: always snoop around your
parents' closet, no matter how square their clothes may
appear. One day those polo shirts and boating shoes are
going to show up in a video and, if you play it right, you'll
be ready before anyone else. As an added bonus, your
parents will think you've somehow bonded with them. Let
them think this – you know different; the rest of the world
knows different – and you'll be afforded hours of new-
found rock-and-roll freedom, satisfied that hanging
around with the squarest people on Earth finally paid off.

The Fabulous Poodles, Etc.

Naming Your Band

Band names mean nothing. Okay, they don't mean nothing, but they mean very little. A group like the Barenaked Ladies benefited from the attention they got for their name, but if they hadn't been able to play, it wouldn't have mattered what they called themselves. Names are interchangeable, but character and quality is not. Nobody ever resisted the music of Neutral Milk Hotel, or Echo and the Bunnymen, or the Traveling Wilburys because they didn't like the name. And even though I spent countless hours in grade-eleven physics class drawing up lists of potential band names, I believe that our sound would have remained the same had we been called Shoot the Neighbours or Bring Home the Beaver (two other names on the list), instead of Rheostatics. Which is a pretty stupid name, if a little less stupid than those we didn't choose.

While there are no rules when it comes to choosing a band name, it's important to avoid certain clichés of the day. Every rock-and-roll epoch has been defined by what musicians called their groups. The 1950s, for instance, was a big time for bands named after birds and cars – the Robins, Orioles, Doves, Nightingales; the Fleetwoods, Cadillacs, GTOs, and Ventures – while '60s group names had the ring of characters from a Lewis Carroll novel: the Electric Prunes, the We Five, the Strangeloves, Blue Magoos, Amboy Dukes, Chocolate Watchband, Sam Sham and the Pharaohs, ? and the Mysterians, 1910 Fruitgum Company, Sir Douglas Quintet, Jefferson Airplane, the Grateful Dead, and the Incredible String Band, to name a few. This, in turn, spawned a movement towards simpler names: Poco, the Byrds, Love, the Band, the Move. As Richard Manuel suggested to Martin Scorsese in *The Last Waltz*, "When we were starting out, all of these bands had names like Chocolate Subway and Marshmallow Overcoat. So we just decided to call ourselves the Band."

The '70s gave way to an onslaught of groups whose names suggested a certain heaviosity of sound: Black Oak Arkansas, Foghat, Grand Funk, T.Rex, Led Zeppelin, Styx,

FIST, Trooper, Motorhead, Black Sabbath, Anvil, Gong,
Bachman-Turner Overdrive (BTO). Parallel trends saw
bands using proper names, often of people not in the band
(Max Webster, Jethro Tull, Barclay James Harvest, Norton
Buffalo), acronyms (ELO, ELP, XTC, PIL, ZZ Top, X, M,
CCR, DOA, and, once again, BTO), and the names of
cities, countries, and occasionally continents (Boston,
Chicago, Toronto, Chilliwack, Chelsea, New England,
Kansas, UK, Europe, and Asia). At the end of the '70s, a
Punk band just wasn't unless its moniker evoked the dread
of modern life: Siouxsie and the Banshees, the Damned,
the Sex Pistols, the Ruts, the Clash, the Slits, the Fall,
Stranglers, the Dead Boys, Black Flag, Killing Joke, Fear, or
Bad Brains.

New Wave bands of the 1980s favored themes of science or
science fiction (the Space Invaders, Devo, Moon Martin,
Wire, the Triffids, Oingo Boingo, Telex), or haughty
globalism (Spandau Ballet, Classix Nouveaux, Depeche
Mode, Duran Duran, Kajagoogoo, Eyeless in Gaza, Scritti
Politti, Erasure, Bauhaus, X-Mal Deutschland, Bolshoi,
Falco, China Crisis, Sigue Sigue Sputnik, Blancmange,
Visage, Japan, Berlin, Cabaret Voltaire). The '90s featured a
litany of numbered bands: Sum 41, Finger Eleven, blink-
182, Matchbox Twenty, NC-17, Six Doors Down, 50 Cent,
Buck 65, Galaxy 500, Nine Inch Nails, Sevendust, Sixpence

None the Richer, Shed Seven, L7, Spacemen 3, Catch 22,
Eve 6, 88 Fingers Louie, 7 Seconds, Mojave 3, Bran Van
3000, Andre 3000, and Powerman 5000, who, by dint of his
name, was clearly at least 2000 better than anyone else.
Most recently, the trend has been towards purposely
misspelled band names (Staind, Linkin Park, Limp Bizkit,
Phish, Outkast), names with the word "Super" in them
(Superconductor, Supergarage, Superchunk, Superdrag,
the Super Friendz, the Supersuckers, Super Furry Animals,
Princess Superstar, Supersonic; strangely, Supertramp
preceded this trend way back in the '70s), or, regrettably,
bands linking the names of celebrities and mass murderers
(Brian Jonestown Massacre, Marilyn Manson).

Then there are animal names. Young bands should
approach this category with caution. It's not that I dislike
many of these groups, but none of them would be
mistaken for the Beatles, the Byrds, or the Animals (or, all
right, the Eagles), which are the exceptions to the Curse of
the Animal Name. Examples include Glass Tiger, Slaughter
and the Dogs, Elephants Memory, Buffalo Tom, the Stray
Cats, White Lion, the Monkees, Faster Pussycat, Hootie
and the Blowfish, the Beaver Brown Band, Kid Koala, Babe
the Blue Ox, Ducks Deluxe, Raising the Fawn, Alien Ant
Farm, Whitesnake, Cats Can Fly, Flock of Seagulls, Budgie,
the Fabulous Poodles, Ratt, Cat Power, Courage of Lassie,

Toto, Mouse on Mars, Cobra, Armadillo, Adam and the
Ants, the Bee People, Spiderbait, the Black Crowes,
Counting Crows, and the Rainbow Butt Monkeys.

Some bands were lucky enough to be named accidentally.
Before the Guess Who were called that – they were
unofficially known as Chad Allen and the Expressions –
they bombarded radio stations with brown paper packages
containing their new single, "Shakin' All Over." In an effort
to stir interest regarding the true identity of the group,
only two words appeared on the sleeve: Guess Who? The
resulting media frenzy never occurred because DJs decided
that it didn't matter who was playing the song. That it
sounded like a bona fide hit was good enough for them, so
they just called the band the Guess Who, even though the
name was strikingly similar to the name of another band
of the time, the Who. The Who and the Guess Who
actually met once, at the Marquee Club in London. The
Who were upset because British audiences kept requesting
"Shakin' All Over," while the Guess Who had been forced
to deal with calls for "My Generation." Randy Bachman,
the Guess Who's guitarist, remembers Pete Townshend
asking the Guess Who to change their name. They told
them to change theirs. Nothing was settled. Rock and roll
was allowed to take its course.

Some bands have changed their names in an effort to distinguish themselves from the pack (Martha and the Muffins became M+M; Spizz Energi became Athletico Spizz 80; John Cougar reinserted his real name, Mellencamp), while many of those who might have considered getting a new handle actually thrived using their own names. Folksinger Loudon Wainwright III, who possesses one of music's most difficult-to-spell names, once arrived at a venue to find *Gordondon Wainwright* written on the marquee. In her early days, Ani Difranco was accidentally billed as Andy Difranco, and Led Zeppelin's name was forever butchered in club and concert listings. My band has also suffered the same fate. Over the years, we've been known as Red Static, Rheostapic, Riostatics, and Reostatics, as well as the constant Rheostat. After a while, I stopped taking it personally, and was happy that we were even listed.

In almost every instance, a band's name will come back to haunt you. It's a label you invent at fourteen that you end up using at forty-four. Very few songs from those early years survive, but a band's name remains. As you get older, it'll sound dated and old, and you'll have trouble saying it in public. But you'll learn to deal with it. There are a lot of other things you'll learn to deal with, too: bored crowds, or no crowds; ugly posters, T-shirts, album covers, and print ads; dumb things you told the press that you thought they wouldn't print, but did; radio DJs who ask stupid stuff like, "How'd you get your name?"; bummer tours, or bad colds, or throat nodes, or breakups with girlfriends/boyfriends in the middle of tours or album sessions; songs that won't hatch, bandmates who won't listen, muses that won't strike when you need them to most. Once you've dealt with all of these things, coming to terms with a stupid band name is the simplest of tasks. You go with it, mostly because you have no choice. Either that, or you rename your group after the author who warned you about this in the first place.

Go on.

I dare you.

The Men Who Hold High Places

Bands We Love and Why

As a kid in love with rock and roll, Rush was the first real band with whom I was obsessed. For those of you who can't place the name, Rush was one of the main influences of Primus, the band who wrote the *South Park* theme. Jack Black also espouses the group's significance in *School of Rock*, and it was the Tragically Hip's Gord Downie who called Rush's live album *Different Stages* one of the greatest live records of all time.

I was partly into Rush because, as a fourteen-year-old, I wanted to appear older – most of the kids two grades above me were into Rush – and partly because, like tobogganing and watching *The Beachcombers*, to follow them was to quietly awaken one's sense of place. Besides, if you weren't into Rush, you were into disco, an impossible choice. When it was broken down along these lines, Rush was the one band every guy in my neighborhood cared about.

Other communities around the world have had an aural equivalent. Ireland has had Thin Lizzy and U2, Scotland has had Nazareth; Wales has had Super Furry Animals. In London, it was T.Rex or Blur; in Manchester, Rod Stewart or Oasis. The Guess Who and the Weakerthans are Winnipeg's own, and so on. With "Lakeside Park" from Rush's *All The World's A Stage* live album (recorded over three nights at Massey Hall), for the first time I identified a local place in a song – not just a song, mind you, but a kick-ass chunk of molten-metal-prog-rock, embellished with rollercoaster drum fills, chiming guitar flurries, and Geddy Lee's Witchie-Poo vocals. In other books, I've stressed the affect that Stompin' Tom Connors has had on my life, but it was Rush – and to a lesser extent, their cousins-in-song Max Webster – who first sang to me about my home.

Ronnie and I were thirteen, and we were both crazy about Rush. I first encountered him while walking down the hallway of my high school. At the time, I was wearing my

T-shirt with *RUSH 1 TORONTO* on it, which I'd had
steam-pressed on in spongy, white letters at the T-shirt
stall in the Albion Mall.

"You like Rush?" he asked me.

"Ya, man, I love Rush."

"Cool. Wanna hang out?"

"'Kay."

Ronnie was a guitar player, and he was way better than I
was. Not only could he play Alex Lifeson's solos note for
note, but he also looked the part: scrawny and skinny-
legged, with long blond hair spilling over his shoulders.
Though Ronnie lived in a bungalow near Silvercreek Park
with his mom and dad, his brother Rob, and two family
sedans, he looked like he'd woken up in a gulch. His face
was moody and drawn without ever having touched dope
or booze or speed, and the way he wore his guitar – a
sunburst Les Paul with white humbuckers and gold knobs
– slung low across his midriff suggested that he'd had it
strapped across his bony shoulder since birth. Ronnie was
the real thing. I was envious of him from the beginning.

Ronnie and I jammed. We sat at the edge of each other's beds on numberless afternoons, watched over by Rush's *A Farewell to Kings* poster – Geddy Lee, Alex Lifeson, and Neil Peart standing arms-crossed in front of a castle, long greasy hair dripping down their backs – and strummed along to our favorite records. Actually, Ronnie did most of the playing. I studied him closely, copping riffs to "Bastille Day," "Temples of Syrinx," and, of course, "Xanadu," Rush's monumental work of oscillating synths, wind chimes, mystical poetry, and fast, hiccuping bass lines. Ronnie and I saw lots of rock shows together – Max Webster at Maple Leaf Gardens, Triumph and Doucette at the Canadian National Exhibition Grandstand – but most importantly, we saw Rush twice, the last time at the Gardens on their *Hemispheres* tour. One of the best moments came during the flashpot blasts in "Closer to the Heart," when the whole crowd came alight, sixteen thousand faces hanging open as Alex, in his fringed monk's robe, *kerrang*ed a D-major chord, his wild eyes obscured by a carwash curtain of hair that whipped across his face as we yowled pangs of delight.

Ronnie and Rob formed a band called Typhoid. When they first told me what they were going to call their group, I was floored. Typhoid. It was the perfect name. I couldn't believe that no one had thought of it before. The first thing they did was splash their logo in paint across a bed sheet, which they hung behind them when they practiced. Back in the '70s, it was very important to have a backdrop or a lit sign. I'm not sure if you've ever heard of bands like Triumph and Taurus, but it was their signs – triggering sirens and pots of belching smoke – that separated them from the rest. A few years before Typhoid, I'd tried forming a group with my cousin – piano, guitar, and drums – but when I suggested that we do a show, he said, "Naw, man, we can't do that. We don't have a sign. We'll just end up playing with some band that has a sign and get blown off the stage."

Typhoid staged concerts in their parents' basement, and the highlight of the show was their last number, the Rush song "Working Man," which featured Robbie's drum solo. Robbie laid it down across roto toms, gongs, and cowbells, and to me it sounded like the end of the world. At solo's end, he threw his sticks into the crowd, which comprised myself, a few cousins, and their parents. Maybe their grandmother. During the show, Ronnie introduced the songs with a vaguely American drawl (which I thought gave him instant rock-and-roll credibility), but most of the time he just stood there in repose, looking messed-up in front of homemade wooden cabinets, enormous blond boxes with small speakers in the center. For each concert, the brothers built more speakers and, while their sound more or less remained the same, their gear got bigger and bigger. It was like something out of Pink Floyd's *The Wall*. After a while, the speakers crowded Robbie and his kit, which expanded too: cymbals added to cymbals, tom rack over tom rack, and finally a double bass drum that, when he played it, blew my mind.

Like a lot of kid friendships, the one between Ronnie and me could not last. With the passing of time, and as we hurdled grades in middle and high school, my ideas about music started to evolve. Soon, I cast off the power chords and glam candy of Metal and hard rock for defiance, rebellion, anger, dread: the sound and ethos of Punk rock. Ronnie got into Punk too, but he hadn't been hit as hard. This drove a wedge between us. It happens. With change, certain people come to represent what you used to be, and this was the case with Ron and Rob for me. I began to find myself looking at those speaker boxes and just shaking my head. I believed that if you didn't buy into what bands like X-Ray Specs and the Damned were about, you were a conformist, and conformists were the enemy of Punks. I made new friends, got into new bands, dressed differently. One weekend, I begged my parents to let me have a New Wave party. They said I could. I didn't invite Ronnie. At the party, two other friends crank called Ronnie's home.

For Tommy and Monk, it was typical behavior. Tommy, in particular, liked to harass the hosts of TV call-in shows. He'd call them up, pretending to be someone he wasn't, and tell them, "I've got a plastic bag over my head!" or "I've got my head in the oven!" It was a wonder that he ever got through and, to a seventeen-year-old, it was hilarious stuff. The next day in school, Tommy was a real hero of the hallways.

At first, I was unaware that Tommy had called Ronnie's parents from my party. Most of the kids were in the basement, dancing to music I'd taped off of Bow Wow Wow, the Demics, and Sex Pistols albums. Ronnie's mom answered the phone, and Tommy and Monk uttered the first thing that came into their heads: "Mrs. W, your sons have been killed in a car accident."

Then they hung up the phone, laughing.

A while later, there was a pounding on the door. When I opened it, Ronnie, Rob, and about five of their friends charged into the hallway. Ronnie waved an X-Acto knife, and he came at me. He slashed the air and screamed my name. He howled something about his mother, how upset she was, and I fell backwards against the stairs, holding up

my hand for Ronnie to stop. It was a bewildering scene.
My friends rushed up from the basement. Kenny Huff
grabbed Ronnie and pushed him out the front door. After
a struggle on the driveway, he climbed back into his car.
He had this strange, twisted look on his face, and as the car
pulled away one of his friends shouted out the window
that he was going to find me after school and break my
fingers. It was terrible. A few days passed and Tommy and
Monk finally confessed to what they'd done. Five years
later, Monk himself died in a car crash.

I thought of Ronnie and Robbie and Typhoid when the
Rheostatics got to record with Neil Peart in 1992. I'd met
rock stars before, but it was special meeting Neil because
he was among my first heroes. I'd actually talked to Neil
once before, having interviewed him by phone for a local
magazine. This was a profound event, too. At the end of
the interview – he'd called in from the Chateau Frontenac
hotel in Old Quebec, and I was bleary-headed from
staying out late the night before – I asked him if he was
listening to any new bands. He paused a minute and said,
"Well, there's this one band from Etobicoke. They're called
the Rheostatics. Have you heard of them?"

"I'm . . . in them," I said, stuttering.

"That song, 'Horses,'" he said. "We were recording and I couldn't get it out of my head. We were doing a track, and I just couldn't concentrate. I was playing the song, but all I could hear was, 'Holy Mackinaw Joe,'" he said. "I had to stop and go out and buy the record."

Neil came down to Reaction Studios while we were making our *Whale Music* album and set up a little yellow jazz kit in the corner. The Barenaked Ladies were there, too; they'd just laid in their background vocal to "California Dreamline" earlier in the day. We all huddled together and watched as Neil warmed up on his kit. Gone was his wild viny hair, fringed robe, and shaggy moustache, but he was still a ghostly figure under the low studio lights. Head lowered, torso centered, feet kicking, his hands glancing over the drums, Neil played all afternoon. We were glued to the carpet, aware that we were listening to one of the greatest drummers in the history of music play. It's one thing to see your hero perform from a faraway seat in Maple Leaf Gardens, but it's something else to be so near his work as I was that day. Once upon a time in my life, I'd dreamed of what it would be like merely to attend a Rush concert; even before that, I'd booked my time after school around a chance to see their video for "Closer to the Heart" on TV. And there I was, sitting on the studio parquet, not twenty feet from where he was crafting a part for a song that would appear on our album.

While Neil played, I thought of Ronnie: how he used to bend the fat strings of his Les Paul to play the vibrato riff of "What You're Doing," his skinny wrists working the neck, his tongue curved over his lip, trying to get the riff just right. And I thought of Rob's drum solo, all flailing arms and slumping meter, the sound of the suburbs, the sound of Rush, and what it had taken for me to be where I was, living this rock-and-roll dream. As Neil commanded his kit, he painted my adolescence before me, evoking everything about it, and even though I sat alone, I imagined that Ronnie was there, too, watching our hero as he played and played and played, tapping out rhythms of the heart for a kid who was once best friends with another kid, and they loved Rush.

A World of Brown and Tan

The Studio

The studio is a crazy place. It's where musicians tap into their most eccentric impulses. Live performances have a certain decorum about them – they are, after all, public presentations – but in the studio, musicians don't have to worry about screwing up or looking bad, or whether their hair's blue or purple. They can experiment without anyone judging their failure, safely harbored from the masses. They can record grand pianos submerged in swimming pools, as one-hit wonder Terence Trent D'Arby did; hire a twenty-piece symphony orchestra to play random notes counted out by a cigar-chomping bodyguard, as the Beatles did; or insist that side musicians wear firemen's coveralls and stand in a sandbox, as Brian Wilson did for *Smile*.

This insanity, creative or otherwise, is a product of a handful of people spending a relatively long period of time together in a relatively small room. Recording is sort of like touring, only you don't go anywhere. As a result, bands find ways to defuse the inevitable tension.

In 1994, the Rheos had the opportunity to record at one of the world's best – and most famous – studios, Compass Point in the Bahamas. Some of the greatest rock records have been recorded there: *Back in Black* by AC/DC, *Uprising* by Bob Marley, the first B-52's album, *Fear of Music* by the Talking Heads, Grace Jones's *Nightclubbin'*, and the later records of the Rolling Stones. The equipment room had amplifiers that ZZ Top and Led Zeppelin once used (I recorded an overdub with a Danelectro guitar combo that Jimmy Page used for *Led Zeppelin 2*), and historic spools of tape were forever falling out of closets. At Compass Point, you could stand on the very spot where Bob Marley sang "Redemption Song." At one point during the session, Ozzie, the engineer's assistant, grabbed the microphone and whispered, "Bob is here . . . Bob is going to make this record very good, very heavy . . ." into our headphones.

Between takes, we'd run from the studio and splash in the froth of the sea that lay just a few feet beyond the doors, which sat kitty-corner to a row of beachside homes owned by Paul McCartney and David Bowie. During our session, which lasted two weeks, we lived in an apartment below the mother of Talking Heads bassist Tina Weymouth, and we regularly encountered her tending her garden. Before we arrived, Jimmy Buffet had just completed a recording in which he'd hosted sixty of his best friends, flying them to and from the island by private jet; upon leaving, we were supplanted by Jon Bon Jovi, who'd booked the $1200-a-day studio to write tracks for his new album.

During our recording, Ozzie told us about Status Quo. Their method of maintaining studio sanity was to rig a tape deck and microphone in the corner of the room. Whenever they were gripped with flatulence, they raced to the machine, pointed their trumpet at the microphone, and delivered. At the end of the recording, they'd play back the tape. Ozzie told us that it was the funniest thing he'd ever heard.

He also described the method Status Quo used to score with the local ladies. In no way am I endorsing this behavior, but in the interests of drawing a complete picture, I feel required to tell you this. The first thing the Quo did upon arriving in town was to run an ad in the local newspaper announcing auditions for young women wanting to appear in a *FAMOUS ROCK BAND'S VIDEO*. Within days, the prospective talent would be lined up outside the door, and, between takes, the group would interview the potential subjects, getting their phone numbers. The women, thrilled to be in the studio's inner sanctum and in the presence of a *real live rock star*, would offer the details of their lives. Intimacy would, inevitably, ensue. The band would leave town once their record was completed, never having intended to shoot a frame of video.

Recording in the Bahamas was a far cry from our first experiences in the studio as teenagers. It's difficult to express the anxiety, fear, and uncertainty that I felt during those first sessions, which were done at an industrial mall in Brampton in a place called Evolution Sound 2000, which I picked out of the phone book. I was terrified the first time I heard my voice and instrument coming back at me on tape. Since this was before the dawn of cheap, fast, excellent home digital recordings, it wasn't often that you got a chance to hear what you sounded like. Not only that, but since our funds – rather our parents' funds – were limited, we recorded with the pressure of knowing that if we didn't get it right, we might not ever get the chance again. Guitarist Dave Edmunds remembers going in the

ROCK TALK
In the Studio

The recording studio is a world of its own, and it has its own language. A *side musician* is a player who isn't officially in the band. He or she supplements the music in the studio without actually writing or *touring* a record. An *overdub* is a performance that's layered on top of the basic, or *bed*, tracks; *tracks* being all instruments, voices, or sound effects within a song that combine like the strands of a rainbow to make a single thick stripe. On the *sound board* or *mixing console*, the engineer can separate these tracks and listen to them either individually or collectively, all the better to *mix*.

studio in England with his band for the first time and recording twelve songs in under an hour, unaware that they were allowed to record more than one take. The opposite would have been true for Ritchie Valens, who sang "La Bamba" sixty-eight times, never really sure if he'd got it right.

Studios are weird because they look like no other places on Earth. They're airless, corduroy corridors, baffled with brown and tan carpets and walls. They're sealed at every crevice and corner so that the sound can be properly contained, and to spend any amount of time there is to feel like an astronaut stranded in the lounge of some spacecraft as imagined in the science fiction of 1974. Because there are no windows – again, for soundproofing – there's never any natural light to remind you of the time of day. In a studio, it's always 4:21 p.m. on a winter afternoon. The year implied often depends on the vintage of equipment used.

In the studio, you're forced to listen to your bandmates through headphones. Headphones are the result of having to isolate instruments to minimize the bleed of one sound into another (instrument bleed makes doing overdubs troublesome). Again, in pre-digital recording days, one hardly ever used headphones to record at home, so it was quite an adjustment to get used to hearing your music compressed into those little shells, to say nothing of the way the headphones felt, perpetually strapped to the head.

I can only imagine what our drummer – at the time, Rod Westlake – suffered, having to set up his drums in an acrylic pod in another requirement of sound isolation. He looked like a guppy in a tank, encased in thick, transparent protection from the rest of the musicians. Drummers feel alone half the time anyway, and the isolation booth only exacerbates this feeling. If that wasn't bad enough, Rod's playing was picked apart after we heard the drum track separated from the rest of the instruments. A drummer's ability, or lack thereof, to keep time tends to be exposed once the song is deconstructed to its most naked elements. When you're jamming or playing live, the immediacy of performance doesn't demand pinpoint time-keeping – one of the hallmarks of many live records is that they speed up and slow down all the time – but in the studio a band's worst tendencies are laid bare as they come through the console. Rod's time was less dependable than we'd thought, and, as a result, the studio's engineer suggested that we play to a click-track. Our trapsman recoiled at the thought, for playing to a click-track, in some cases, is like pouring concrete into a musician's veins.

A click-track is a robotic rhythm inserted into the recording so that the musicians have an unwavering tempo to follow. Some bands (the Who, for one) forgo rhythmic accuracy, while others (like the Police) value it. The click-track might seem like a practical – even ingenious – solution to recording (and, in a way, it is), but in some cases it can shackle a drummer's playing, deadening the spirit of the performance by demanding singular devotion to the drummer's abilities to keep perfect time, as opposed to letting the looseness and spirit of rock and roll carry the

day. Most bands try for a bed track of the rhythm
instruments before inserting guitars, keyboards, and, later,
vocals, so drums and bass are almost always singled out in
the early parts of recordings. It's easy for a band to get
obsessed with getting the drummer's part exactly right. In
the throes of creating art, this is not the idea at all. Ideally,
what you want to do is get a take that feels right – a slight
waver in time be damned – so that the rest of the band can
be themselves in subsequent overdubs.

Despite our rookie trials in the studio, I brought home a
cassette tape of our first session and played it over and
over. I thought it was the greatest music ever, although,
listening to it now, it sounds mildly hilarious. Still, I sent
the tape out to a few small, local record companies, and
one of them, Ready Records, wrote back to tell us that,
while they weren't signing any more bands that year, they'd
be eager to hear whatever else we did. Of course, we took
this as a ringing endorsement of our craft. It's not unlike
how April Wine felt upon receiving a rejection letter from
a Montreal label, which told them, "If ever you're in town,
please drop by and see us!" The next week, the band took
off to *la belle province*, where they showed up at the offices
of Aquarius Records expecting to start work on an album
for their new label.

A few years after our experiences at Evolution Sound 2000, we went into another studio. At Round Sound, a second engineer replaced the first in mid-session. The second fellow was a large, bearish man who mostly grunted. I remember him ordering a party-sized pizza and laying it across the console, right over the knobs he was supposed to use to tweak and sharpen our sounds. We recorded and mixed two songs in a single day. It became our first record.

It wasn't until we recorded at a place called Comfort Sound with producer Doug McClement that I fully understood the potential of a studio. Doug was the first person I met who didn't just have us plug in and play. Instead, he obsessed over microphone placement, especially on the drums, experimenting with sounds and distances and arrangements of the baffles. I heard our sound change and come alive before my very eyes – or ears – finally understanding, at nineteen, that studios are places where you're allowed to manipulate, sharpen, stretch, and color sounds the way you never can on stage. In the studio, it's possible to diagram a sound to suit your desires, using myriad aural constructions to match the requirements of a particular song. As an artist, Doug possessed the same kind of spirit and sense of play that the Rheos bring to our songs and performances. Before, I'd always thought that engineers or producers were quiet guys who twiddled knobs and ate pizza; I discovered that, while a strong poker face allows them to be objective amid an artist's tempest, it doesn't mean that they can't do their job with a sense of wonder and discovery.

In a way, producers have to be as free-minded as the band they're recording. On the song "Dear God" by XTC, you'll notice that the first verse is sung by a child. When the group originally tracked the tune, singer Andy Partridge sang all of the verses. Then one morning he showed up to find a small girl warbling into a huge microphone in the middle of the room. He confronted producer Todd Rundgren, outraged at what he was seeing. Rundgren just held up his hands. He'd brought in the girl to give the song a quality of naivete to reflect the lyrics. Partridge, of course, hated what Rundgren had done, yet "Dear God" is among XTC's best, best-known, and most interesting songs.

All producers should have a little bit of mad scientist in them. For one of the songs that we recorded at Compass Point, I wanted us to sound like we'd popped out of a music box. Michael Phillip-Wojewoda, our producer (as well as producer of Jane Siberry, the Barenaked Ladies, Great Big Sea, and Spirit of the West), considered the notion, then came up with an idea to make it work. He

made us play at one-eighth speed so that, sped up, our
dirge-like singing became the voices of tiny sprites. On
another tune, we wanted the singer to sound as if he was
singing against a rising storm. After a bit of head-
scratching, Mike appeared one day with a box of Lego, two
giant pieces of Bristol board, and a plank of wood, which
we waggled and slapped to create the soundscape of a
dock rocking in a gale. Another time, he wanted a
particularly nasty tone from Martin's guitar, so he slashed
one of Martin's speakers with a knife (consulting Martin
first, of course). Because you trust a producer with your
art, you have to let them go down the creative road in
hopes that they'll help realize your sonic vision. While this
usually works (as with George Martin and the Beatles),
sometimes it does not (as with Phil Spector and the
Beatles). Choosing the right person to work the board is
essential to making a great record. There's nothing worse
than spending time in a small place with a person you
suspect is sabotaging your art. This was the case with
Partridge and Rundgren. To this day, XTC's leader finds
listening to the album *Skylarking* impossible.

In a way, recording an album is a series of trying moments
that, once completed, pays off in something that your ears
simply can't believe, especially if your producer has just the
right touch. It's a little like working for hours in a kitchen,

then later sitting down to a delicious feast. In the case of
multi-track recordings (as opposed to live, two-track
efforts) drummers are put through six- or seven-hour
drum checks, which are as painful to listen to as they are to
play: *THUMPTHUMPTHUMP! BOAWMBBOAWMB
BOAWMB! PLSHHH! SHRRANNGG!!* Since most albums
are played on a single kit, the engineer/producer labors
over the sound, making the drummer feel as giddy with
self-importance as with ear-weariness and fatigue. For the
rest of the band, it's a deflating false-start to the day,
arriving full of hope and excitement only to sit on the
couch, flipping through old audio magazines until the
drummer is finished hitting things.

If you are a bassist or guitarist, one of your first duties is to
hide your amp in a closet. Or lock it in a box, under a
blanket, or behind a wall of beige baffles (I actually know a
singer – John Samson of the Weakerthans – who sang an
entire album locked inside a square cabinet). Once your
rig is wired through headphones, the sound transforms,
often at the expense of fidelity. The studio is the first place
in your rock-and-roll life where you're not standing in
front of your cabinet, sweating into your treble knob.
Instead of feeling the speakers' heat at your elbows and
knees, headphones tame your *kerrang*. Or at least they
contain it. Part of recording is trusting that whoever is

mixing the sound will be able to draw out the energy of
your performance through the board, no matter how
weird and foreign and plain it sounds in the headphones.

Most bands are required to pretzel into new configurations
in order to serve the aural demands of the studio. I've done
lots of overdubs sitting in a chair or on a couch, playing
riffs that were born in the passion of a scissor-kick. I hate
to smash the fantasy for you, but a lot of your favorite raw-
nerved, head-scalping rave ups were done while the band
was sitting down, their headphones falling over their faces
as they stared at their shoes. And if they didn't get it that
time, they did it again. And again. Rock-and-roll history
has shown us a few exceptions – John Lennon sang "Twist
and Shout" shirtless, after downing a quart of milk to fight
back an encroaching cold; both Zappa and Jimi Hendrix
included live jams on their recordings – but for the most
part, bed-track rock and roll is about as kinetic as an
evening shift at the garage-door factory.

It's in the overdub stage that recordings start to get fun
and take off. With the Rheos, once we've got the beds done
we sit back, listen, and rub our hands together excitedly as
we consider how we might paint the darned thing. Not to
flatter us in particular, but it's a little like Picasso staring at
a sketch and wondering how he might fully bring it to life.

With our producer, we'll kick around ideas starting from
the craziest (Are the Harmonicats still around?) to the
more sober (How about a dash of acoustic guitar?). It's
hard to give you examples of this if you don't have prior
knowledge of our music (so I suggest that you put down
this book, run to your nearest record store, and fill your
satchel with the complete Rheostatics catalogue) but, in
the case of a song like "Me and Stupid" from *Introducing
Happiness*, we mixed in accordion, bits of poetry from a
spoken-word album, two acoustic guitars, a sample from a
Rheos recording circa 1980, and three tracks of Tim
making loon sounds with his hands. On another tune,
"Earth/Monstrous Hummingbirds," we used the tick-
tocking of a grandfather clock, the buzz of a small jet
plane, a vibraphone, some whistling, a few vintage
synthesizers, a mouth trombone choir, and, for the pièce
de résistance, the sound of a baby raccoon feeding, which
we got from a wildlife record.

The record was made in the Bahamas, overdubbed at
Grant Avenue Studios in Hamilton, Ontario, and mixed in
Toronto. If you don't know, "mixing" means exactly that:
measuring and combining all of the elements of the
sessions until the desired balance of song and sound is
achieved. Often, the bass player has whispered in the
producer's ear, "More bass," only to leave the room so that

the drummer can surreptitiously turn up the kick drum. Mixing is about sonically ordering a band's sound, but it's also about splashing an extra layer of paint where desired. For *Introducing Happiness*, clusters of inexplicable (inexplicable to me, that is) outboard gear – noise reduction units, reverbs, effects strips, tape delays, digital delays – were hired to give the record a heightened sound. All told, the album, with all of its bells and whistles, cost more money to make than we'd spent in our entire lives. Knowing what we know now, we might have slushed some of that money aside, rented a cheaper studio and pocketed the cash. The album was budgeted at $140,000.

We spent it all.

Record-Rack Odyssey

Married to the Music

J ust around the corner from Ken Jones Music at the Westway Plaza was Westway Bowl – it was in this bowling alley that the Rheostatics did our first-ever photo shoot, each of us standing with one foot in the lane, the other in the gutter – and, next to Westway Bowl, Beckers Milk. I spent almost as much time hanging around Beckers as I did going to school. For me, the main feature of the store was a record rack that stood near the magazine stand. In it, I found all the latest jazz, blues, and country releases mixed in with the various K-Tel packages. On weekend afternoons, my friends and I, addled on chocolate milk and licorice, stood reading the albums' liner notes and track listings, considering the exotic band names – Big

Brother and the Holding Company? The Pretty Things?
Five Man Electrical Band! The Holy Modal Rounders?! –
while in the throes of another Pixy Stix high.

In many ways, Beckers legitimized the record-buying
experience to my parents, for whom it was no easy task to
stride into a music shop that was decorated with
psychedelic posters and cranking Blue Cheer. Since
Beckers was also the place where they bought milk and
bread, artists like James Gang and Laura Nyro and the Sir
Douglas Quintet were somehow validated. A lot of these
bands were also collected on K-Tel's mainstream, best-of
compilations, like *Sound Explosion* and *Canadian Mint*
(the precursors to records like *Big Shiny Tunes*), and
through them our entire family was exposed to progressive
music. I remember gathering around the stereo and
listening to *I Believe in Music* for the first time, my dad
stoking the fire, Mom sewing, my sister and me buzzing
with delight to the Incredible Bongo Band, Focus, and Al
Green. Another time, we stopped at the plaza on our way
home from a family trip and bought *22 Explosive Hits*, and
I heard Parliament, Loudon Wainwright III, and James
Brown for the first time.

Other than what I found at Beckers Milk, the beginnings of
my record collection – which today numbers in the

ROCK TALK
Before CD

In olden days, records were made of vinyl ("wax") and could be played at varying speeds: 45, 33, or 78 rotations per minute (rpm). Each record played on both sides – A and B – and so did a *cassette tape*, unlike an *8-track*, which was a wallet-size parcel of plastic that hurt when your sister threw it at your head.

thousands – were 45 rpm singles purchased at various malls around the suburbs. I'd like to say that these discs reflected a budding musical sophistication, but unless you regard Jim Croce as some sort of forgotten Mozart of the fretboard, my early tastes were shaped by the pop Top Forty, for better or worse. Occasionally, a song like Edgar Winter's "Frankenstein" or "Live and Let Die" by Paul McCartney and Wings would show up to dignify my wax stack, but for the most part, if I wasn't listening to the DeFranco Family or Bread, I was wigging out to the Andrea True Connection or the Bee Gees. Though embarrassed that my early taste showed a disturbing affinity for effete HappyPop, it's unrealistic to expect that I'd start out the same way as little Frank Zappa, whose teenage musical hero

was the modern classical composer Edgar Varèse. Zappa
discovered Varèse's work at a local electronics shop – the
album had a picture of a mad scientist on the cover – and,
beguiled by the image, he convinced his parents to buy him
the album, which he listened to, day and night, for most of
his young life. One year, his folks asked him what he
wanted for his birthday, and he told them, "To speak with
Edgar Varèse." His parents tracked down the elusive
composer's phone number and, on his fourteenth birthday,
Zappa spoke with his hero.

Beckers fostered my lifelong love of record stores. As a
future touring musician, you'll come to value the
importance of these places as they relate to maintaining
one's sanity and stability on the road. Record stores – at
least the good ones – are vibrant places filled with young
people married to music. In the past, they've even doubled
as recording studios, and still function as impromptu live
venues (country music, Tex-Mex, and border soul started
out in these depots). They're often the cultural and social
nerve centers for local musical communities, not to
mention the coolest places in town. If you ever want to
know what's happening, record stores are perfect
barometers of the local scene. They're the first places I visit
while on tour.

Record store clerks never hassle the touring musician, because they understand the importance of seeking sanctuary away from the madness of the rock-and-roll world; in fact, many are young men and women who've toured themselves. Racks of books and records are excellent places to Zen-out under quiet waves of words or music. If you are a new band on tour, chances are the local record store is the only place in town where people will know your name, graciously pin up a poster, treat you respectfully, and have an appreciation for life on the road, for the trials of being a musician. Ask them, and they might let you do an in-store concert to promote the show. This measure of compassion can go a long way if you are lost in the wilderness of touring, whether you're playing stadiums or chicken-wing bars, rank clubs or bar mitzvahs.

These days, good record stores are as much like libraries as anything. The rebirth of the listening post – a descendant of the listening booth of the 1950s, where kids locked themselves away in acoustically sealed pods and spun stacks of new releases – makes it possible for the music fan to hear hours of music. I'm not promoting loitering here – well, maybe creative loitering – but the concept that, in contemporary record stores, you're likely to soak up more interesting sounds than you'll ever hear on commercial radio, or read about in the mainstream press. People who

work in record stores make it their business to be on top of
the very latest bands. Even in record chains in small towns
where the front racks reflect what they're playing on the
local dance station, there are titles lost in the bins that are
simply waiting to be drawn out. Even the worst record
store wants to sell stuff. Getting the clerk to audition a
new, strange record for you helps everyone.

I have a personal attachment to a number of record stores.
In my youth, I frequented a place called The Record
Peddlar on Queen Street East in Toronto. Every Friday
evening, my friends and I would take the Kipling 45 bus
south to the subway station. In the winter and spring, you
could feel Lake Ontario as it got closer, especially at night
when the moisture clung to your neck and throat. When I
think of Toronto, I think of sitting beside an open window,
tasting the cold and watching the yellow streetlights
swoosh past us like checkmarks, the rest of the evening's
passengers sitting stiff as stumps, many of them half-
asleep, holding Eaton's bags, pawing an old, feathered
newspaper. An old man in a tweed cap. The bored driver
in drab brown. And us, flying above it all.

With the subway depositing us downtown, we soon found
ourselves wandering the record store, listening to the staff
spin 45 after 45, many of which they'd cracked out of a

crate sent from England, New York, or Europe. The store
vibrated with excitement and energy, and the staff was as
young as its patrons, though it was not without a
managerial guru – the late Dave Smeltzer – whom I asked
about Pere Ubu, the Residents, and Love, sophisticated
bands that I graduated to post-New Wave. At The Record
Peddlar, we moved to the pulse of worldwide youth, for it
was probable that other great rock-and-roll stores around
the globe were spinning the same cool records that had
been delivered that day, too. The Ramones might have sold
50,000 copies of their album *Leave Home*, but chances are,
they sold them all in the same kind of shop. When the
Rheostatics finally put out our first single in 1980, Smeltzer
took ten of the little, green-labeled disks on consignment.
I'll never forget the day that they played "Satellite
Dancing" in the store, putting us right in the continuum
of the amazing bands whose sound had shaped our own,
against whom we now leaned, sleeve-to-sleeve, in the *New
Releases* singles rack.

I have many acquaintances in record stores across Canada.
Having visited these places ten, twenty times over the last
few decades, I've developed a relationship with them
beyond artist–salesclerk protocol. Cool record stores get
behind your albums even when the press dries up, the
radio turns its back, or fan support drops. You can always

count on a good record store to hang a poster, hold a contest, promote an album. Even though the Rheos have grown and morphed and aged, many of these stores have held firm, remaining steadfast in their commitment to rock and roll.

The last time we played in Moncton, New Brunswick, the Leger brothers opened the doors to their store – Full Blast – after hours so that we could browse the racks, pick up a few things for the tour. It was something I'd always dreamed about as a teenager: having the run of a great record store; in fact, it sort of made me feel like I'd made it. After putting on the new Yo La Tengo album, the brothers disappeared into the back room, then returned with handfuls of albums that they thought might interest us. I left with a dozen records under my arm, including a bunch of CDs that we played in the van as we navigated the Maritimes, filling those endless hours on the humming road with thrilling new sounds that propelled us to fight on in our battle against bad music.

Radio On

The Airwaves

When Sly Stone was a DJ in San Francisco, he grew weary of having to interrupt the flow of music for pre-recorded commercials. He complained to his station manager and a compromise was reached: the ads would stay, as long as Sly worked them into the show however he saw fit. At his request, a Fender Rhodes keyboard was installed in the booth, and Sly ended up singing the ads. He vamped, riffed, and improvised music while pitching for TV dinners, local car dealerships, and furniture stores; he even promoted upcoming area concerts by performing part of the bands' repertoires. It was the kind of thrilling, speedy aural theater that rock-and-roll radio used to be.

Not to sound like too much of an old crank here, but there are three things that were great when I was growing up, and aren't anymore: pro sports, Hollywood, and commercial radio. In leagues like the NHL, there's too much money, too many teams, and too few characters to sustain drama and intrigue over an entire season; Hollywood is no longer the haven for artists that it was in the 1970s; and commercial radio was long ago hijacked by consultants and media conglomerates who push pre-programmed playlists and homogenous announcers, blanching the wildly expressive environment in which radio once thrived.

In the beginning, rock-and-roll radio was notorious for the way it resembled the music that it played: unpredictable, breakneck, loud, unapologetically robust, enthusiastic, and youthful. The announcers – among them 1950s legends Murray "the K" Kaufman and Alan Freed – were noted for their resistance to convention and mental balance. They carved out their reputations by breaking broadcast rules, whether it meant playing "Blue Moon" by the Marcels twenty-six times in a row, or perching atop a billboard to promote their radio shows. Murray the K's value as a scene-maker was such that he accompanied the Beatles on their first tour of America. Before Beatles manager Brian Epstein brought the group over, he was advised to curry favor with Kaufman, whose radio show dictated the tastes of young New Yorkers.

Many have suggested that the downfall of the great DJs of the '50s was the invention of the Top Forty, a list of oft-repeated hit tunes, but compared to what we hear on radio now, the Top Forty would sound free-form. These days, most announcers are glorified music clerks whose tastes are wedded to playlists and song rotations set by program directors who answer to station managers, station managers who answer to corporate heads, and corporate heads who answer to advertisers. Strict playlisting – it's more like Top Twenty these days – predetermines the number of times a song is played, what kind of song is played, and when. The era of announcers impulsively diving into the record library to reach for a song is a distant memory. I've had announcers tell me that there are only three Rheostatics songs (out of eleven albums) that they're sanctioned to play. There's very little spontaneity in modern commercial radio because DJs are required to maintain a certain order and propriety in programming. And order and propriety are, historically, the enemies of rock and roll.

In older times, a DJ would "break" a record (turn it into a hit) because he or she really liked it. Nowadays, a song has

to meet board approval to get airplay. Most modern radio
– the format is called New Rock in Canada, Triple A in the
U.S. – plays only music made in the last twenty years.
Equally confounding is Classic Oldies radio (the Music of
the '50s, '60s, '70s, and '80s) which repeats the same songs
throughout the day, as if there hasn't been enough good
music over those four decades to freshen daily
programming. A friend of mine who works for a New
Rock station once lamented that, while he couldn't play
Bob Dylan, he could play the Smashing Pumpkins
covering Fleetwood Mac. Modern rock radio provides the
listener with little sense of history or depth in its
programming. Each band is treated as a lonely Sputnik
who, as soon as a few years have passed, is orbited off the
playlist, turning to digital dust in the recesses of the
programmer's laptop.

There's a station called CFNY FM in Toronto (a.k.a. EDGE
radio), which used to broadcast out of an old house in the
nearby suburb of Brampton. The first time the Rheos
went there, to drop off a tape for their annual local band
contest, the person sitting on the front steps was station
manager David Marsden. Marsden won his reputation in
Toronto as Dave Mickey, one of those hiccup-voiced '50s
DJs, but he'd gone on to turn CFNY into an '80s
bellwether for progressive radio. As late as 1989, DJs played

cassette tapes of local bands, opened their microphones to callers, and hosted radio events that brought attention to exciting new bands. They were accessible to fans and musicians alike. Today, however, the front entrance of CFNY's downtown boutique studio is manned by a monolithic security guard with an earring, who stands behind a bolted glass door. The DJs work out of offices in a skyscraper thirty-six floors above. With the exception of one hour of late-night local music programming per week, and the Punk and Metal shows, you won't hear your band on the radio unless you've already signed a record deal.

Since this book is not about yours truly venting his spleen over the demise of rock-and-roll radio, here's the good news that, thankfully, follows the bad: the radio band has never been wider and more diverse.

In Canada, the Canadian Broadcasting Corporation has always been a friend of Canadian bands. One of the Rheos' greatest career boosts came after receiving a postcard written by David Wisdom, who used to host a late-night show called *Nightlines*. David told us, unsolicited, how much he liked our debut album, and how important it was for us to keep doing what we do. When you're a self-conscious young person playing in relative obscurity with a weird band, that sort of support from an important

member of the media is pure gold. Enough of a
relationship developed between the Rheos and *Brave New
Waves*, the CBC's late-night staple showcase of new music,
that when the show's host, Brent Bambury, decided to take
a few months off during the summer, I was called in for an
audition as his temporary replacement. I traveled to
Montreal by train, recorded a dummy show, and – lo and
behold – got the gig. A few weeks later, I was talking to the
whole of Canada.

College radio is even more free-thinking than the CBC.
When musicians who were there at the dawn of rock radio
talk about what it was like, they might as well be
describing college radio. Edmonton pop producer Barry
Allen remembers that, in the 1960s,

> Whatever town you were in, you'd naturally gravitate
> to the radio station. When you did a gig, the first thing
> you did was hire a DJ to MC the show. Right away,
> you became friends with these guys. They were busy
> promoting the scene and the bands, and they couldn't
> wait for your record to come out. They'd move all
> across the country, and if you heard that your record
> was getting played in, say, Moncton, you knew that it
> was because one of these DJs had got a job out there
> and had taken word about the band with them.

Nowadays, stations are insular and the formats are tight.
Radio stations want to be part of the community, but
they're not really; they're so busy playing the big stuff that
they can't be bothered to play the little band that's starting
up, the one that lives in their community.

Ricky Patterson, the veteran Ottawa drummer, recalls,

> The Esquires would get into the town we were
> playing, make a phone call, and nine times out of ten
> you'd get the DJ who was on the air. You wouldn't get
> a receptionist or answering machine. Then you'd say,
> "Hey, we're the Esquires. We're playing in town
> tonight. Can we bring you a copy of our record?" and
> they'd say, "C'mon ahead." You'd walk in and there'd
> be no guards, no special buttons to push; you'd go
> right in, sit with the DJ; they'd spin your record, talk
> about the gig. Today, that's an impossibility. You may
> not fit the station's format. It would mean going on
> the air without being screened.

Since campus radio depends on annual fundraising drives,
there are no sponsors to placate. DJs are allowed to play
what they want, when they want. When Stompin' Tom
Connors was on tour a few years ago, he opened the
Calgary phone book and, disguising his voice, called every

radio station in town to request one of his songs. His plea
fell on deaf ears until the DJ at CJSW, the University of
Calgary's campus station, honored his request,
interrupting an electro-dance program to spin one of the
Stomper's Canadian country chestnuts.

College stations are great places to boil in the music of the
moment, surrounded by a flood of new records, with local
and international bands filing through the door to be
interviewed and young people like yourself determined to
express their love and devotion to rock and roll. Further to
that, a lot of campus stations have their own music
journals, fanzines, or the online equivalent, with most of
the articles written by the DJs themselves. In late summer,
college stations usually appeal to the community for
volunteers, though students can apply at the beginning of
each school year. In any case, they're accessible and easy to
find, with nary an earring'ed security ape blocking the
unbolted doorway.

These days, a lot of campus stations broadcast online,
which brings us to another alternative to modern rock
radio: the Internet. When AM radio was born, kids asked
themselves how they'd ever lived without it; when FM
supplanted AM – bringing with it album rock and playing
entire sides of records, if not Iron Butterfly's "Ina Gadda

Da Vida" every two hours – the reaction was the same.
Now that Internet radio has established itself, fans are
hard-pressed to imagine a musical landscape without
endless digital libraries at their disposal.

It's now possible to experience bands you've heard of from
countries you never knew existed, accessing the indigenous
music of, say, Burkina Faso, through websites, online radio
stations, or one of the many file-sharing or music download
services. Musicians can now reach vast listening publics
around the world without having to rely on the one cool
radio station in Taos, New Mexico, or Cardiff, Wales, to play
their music. The Rheos get e-mail all the time from people
in faraway places who've discovered us through the
Internet.

I'm not going to sit here and suggest ways to establish what
the eggheads call a "web presence" – Rheostatics websites
have been up and down affairs, and it was only recently that
I traded in my clunking gray computer for a sporty laptop
and high-speed connection – but the ability to reach an
infinite fan base makes getting one's music online sort of
essential in our epoch. It still happens the old way, of course
– great live bands make their own loyal audiences, etc. – but
while I used to discover music by flipping wildly up and

down the radio dial, I now apply this technique to music
sites and file-sharing programs, tapping in to a flood of
sounds, new and old.

But, as you've probably heard, there's a catch to all of this.
In Canada, songwriters are protected by a federal copyright
law, which basically says that a radio station can't play your
record without paying for it. This law, however, does not
apply to the Internet; as a result, scores of listeners are
downloading music for free. Tons of artists have, naturally,
come out against free music downloading; very few have
stood up in support of it. Most, like yours truly, are
probably torn between wanting to get paid for their
recordings while maintaining the right to surf unbound,
collecting music from multiple sources that they might not
hear were they required to slide a coin into the jukebox
every time. In many ways, online music is a glorious
listening post. It's a great laboratory where the music fan
can test certain bands and sounds, and decide whether or
not to pledge allegiance. What happens after that is the real
issue. Do you download the rest of the band's catalog, or do
you visit your favorite record store and buy the new album?
Do you conscientiously sign up to a pay site where money
is shared among musicians and their publishers, or do you
park your guilt and take a free ride instead?

It's a tough choice. I think that indiscriminately protesting free downloading is hypocritical for any musician who loves music. Musicians who love music would be crazy to ignore what is, potentially, the greatest free music resource the Earth has ever known. To simply turn away either means that a) the artist is lying, or b) he or she doesn't love music enough. For anyone with a passion for sound, it's impossible to resist that which modern technology has given us, provided you have the means to acquire the necessary equipment.

Still, does this mean bands should just give it away? Its a complicated matter. Carpenters should be paid for making deck chairs just as John Bonham should get paid for playing "Moby Dick," all sixteen minutes of it. To exclude musicians from this equation would be to greatly devalue music. Commercial radio has done enough to devalue it already, using it as listening bait to sell cars and fitness programs. But, at the same time, it's only a handful of artists who ever see money from record sales, anyway. In general, musicians' earnings come from radio airplay royalties, publishing, and live receipts. Royalty rates on record sales are bizarrely low (our last contract paid us somewhere around two dollars per album); record companies claim this is necessary to pay for sales staff, publicity, distribution, and the company's receptionist. All of these people work to make the record-business wheel spin, even though without music and musicians there'd be no spokes or spindle.

So, if the artist makes little money from record sales, what does it matter if I download the new British Sea Power record for free? As a musician, would I rather have someone download my record, burn it, then rush out and pay fifteen dollars (of which I earn at least half) to see me play, or not hear me at all? Of course, I'd choose the former. On the other hand, if no one ever left their home to go down to their record store to buy our CDs, would we still have the confidence to make them? There's something to be said about seeing one's album leap off the shelves, or people coming up to you after shows with CD covers to sign. With unlimited downloading, there'd be none of that. Every band would exist in the same yawning vacuum.

We hear a lot from record companies about how downloading is killing the business. I wonder whether the record business would be in trouble had prices for their product not doubled as the industry flipped from vinyl records to CDs in the early 1990s. With a sexy new technology to sell, labels were able to charge a grossly inflated price for disks. But as the novelty of the new medium wore off, more and more people started to weigh the wisdom of investing that much money in something that had once cost them half the amount. With the birth of free music, it was unreasonable to think that the greater public would go back to habitually buying records.

Not to chew too long on this bone, but lowering the price of CDs is one of the ways the public might be drawn back into record stores, at least the big chain stores (good independent stores will always have a devoted clientele). Folks of my generation remember a day when you could come home from Sam's on Yonge Street with five records for thirty dollars, but a lot of people today are lucky if they buy ten CDs a year. Really, if most people were given the option of playing by the industry's rules, or investing in a computer with a high-speed Internet connection to have thousands of titles suddenly at their disposal, it doesn't take a financial genius to know what route they'd take. What's ironic is that the kind of diverse music and unbiased programming found on the Internet was once part of our everyday rock-and-roll culture. People had a stunning array of sounds that cost nothing to hear.

It was called the radio.

From Sea to Shining Sewer

Going on Tour

Most of my rock-and-roll touring has been done in Canada, which is to say, in the winter. Touring Canada is adventure travel. Those contestants on *Survivor* wouldn't last a week in an unheated van hurtling across the ice-encrusted prairie in January. The first time the Rheostatics played in the U.K., our road manager told us, before retiring to her room, "Okay, we'll meet in the lobby at noon for our drive to the next gig." It seemed absurd to have to travel fewer than six or seven hours to the next city, through a weatherscape lacking marauding winds and snow. In Canada, not only are musicians required to fight the industry's narrow passageways and challenging geographic trade routes to get from city to city, but you must do battle with the screaming elements for five or six months out of twelve if you're to play at all.

Still, it's a lot better to record guitars in the winter than in the summer, producer Michael Phillip-Wojewoda has suggested, in another absurd example of how Canadian bands have come to embrace that which has long tried to kill them. Despite black-ice carpets and frost-clawed trees, many songwriters have paused to find beauty in the terrible menace of winter. Joni Mitchell, balled up in the crook of her divan by gentle Californian moonlight, wished she had frozen river to skate away on. In "Alberta Bound," the dirty city snow is not quite true enough for Gordon Lightfoot; he needs a wailing Grande Prairie gale to face the day. "The Coldest Night of the Year" is Bruce Cockburn's excuse for a love song. In "Acadian Driftwood," the Band's exiled Acadians long for the taste of frost in the sultry heat of the bayou. Rush wrote "By-Tor and the SnowDog."

Yup, weird.

Once, in 1992, the Rheos found ourselves in Drumheller, Alberta. We'd decided to divert our rock-and-roll tour for a look at the famous dinosaur museum, but the place was closed by the time we arrived. On our way there, we noticed groups of small people with strange, hairy faces

tromping through the snow; I'd forgotten that it was
Halloween. When we arrived at the empty park, a few of
the guys got out of the bus – driven by our Australian road
manager, Richard Burgman, his switchblade eyes taking in
the desolation of the place – only to press their noses
against the cold glass for a long look at the old bones.

Then, they disappeared. They became engulfed in a roar of
snow and ice, and it wasn't even November. Richard sat in
the driver's seat and told Australian cannibal stories –
Richard liked to tell Australian cannibal stories – as my
bandmates vanished in the chilling haze. I turned on the
radio in an attempt to mute his tales of bone-eating and
skin-stripping, but the signal was intermittent. Above us,
the bus antenna whipped and *poing*ed in the wind. When
the signal finally came through, it settled on a CBC news
broadcast: a rescue team had been dispatched to assist the
passengers of a small plane downed in Alert. They'd been
stranded there for four days. Time was running out.

I imagined the survivors sitting in the cold, the specter of
cannibalism lurking among them. In the cabin behind us,
Tim prepared a rock-and-roll feast of barely-toasted bread
with a knife-length of peanut butter. He told us,
concerned, "We should really get some more supplies for
this trip." After the wind settled, the guys returned to the

bus. Eventually, we pressed on, driving into the teeth of the storm to Red Deer, where, at Mortimer's Nightclub in the Capri Hotel, we played to four people.

Gigging in the winter isn't the worst thing that can happen to a touring musician – not being invited to tour is a lot worse – because, in their own way, winter gigs can be more glorious than those performed in the mellow summer. There's a lot to be said for playing a packed club in deep July, but winter gigs are always a little more memorable. Just being in a hot place when it's minus-eighteen degrees outside gives fans and musicians cause to rejoice. The heat and power of the music have an immediate effect on a crowd, thrilled to be there in spite of cars that didn't start, subway tracks that froze, sidewalks that robbed them of their footing, and driveways blocked by lumpen snowbanks. In the winter, every gig is an oasis, every fan a symbol of cultural defiance. When you arrive at a warm club or theater, you've already been stimulated by the elements, your senses goosed awake. Lazy summer crowds are fine and easy, but winter crowds keen and lurch towards you, drawn to your sound like moths to a light.

The first time we played in Sydney, Cape Breton, we arrived just after nightfall at a club called Chandler's,

named, regrettably, after the character from the TV show
Friends. Chandler's is a tavern with tile floors, old wooden
tables, and a small stage that has the front window of the
club as its back wall. After setting up our gear, we were
taken to our dressing room in the dark, moldy basement
of the bar. No sooner had we sat down than a gush of gray
water burst from a pipe in the ceiling. It sprayed us,
dousing our clothes, including the only item of winterwear
– a wool sweater – that Martin had brought on the January
tour. I excused myself and told the guys I was going to the
hotel. When I got there, I ordered a hamburger that had
bits of green in the meat. I turned on the television to find
an episode of Ken Burns's *Jazz*, in which Charlie Parker
leaves a train to wander alone in the desert looking for
heroin, then dies.

I trudged back through the frozen streets, head down,
heart sunk. When I opened the door to the club, I was
assaulted by heat. Inside, there were four hundred kids,
some of them swinging from the ceiling pipes. It was an
incredible gig. We played for hours, and then more, and
then more still. Later on, we went to a party at a big house
right next to Rita MacNeil's. One of us fell asleep in a
closet. I walked home laughing like a goof at the brutal,
blue cold.

Every Canadian band has a story about touring in the winter. Here's one of my diary entries about touring in Alberta:

> We're swamped by monstrous snowfall, a white wall of wind and savage cold that threatens to shut down the province's main north-south arrow of a highway. Gary Stokes, our soundman, bites his lip and holds the steering wheel like he's working the horns of a bull. The blizzard kicks the sides of the van like a band of rampaging thugs. We pass rows of ditched cars, some of them buried under huge churches of snow, their side mirrors sticking out like frostbitten hands signaling for help. We hunch to look out under the frostline of the front window and see nothing but cars shimmying wildly across lanes, rebelling against years of drivers moving them in straight lines. A copsickle standing outside an emergency cruiser that paints the snowbanks with blue light, waves his mitten at us. We skid, but can't stop, so he windmills us through and we inch closer, slow as erosion, southbound to Calgary.

Geddy Lee once told me a story about Rush's early days:

> We were playing in either Melville or Estevan, Saskatchewan; I can't remember which. We were

scheduled to play at the arena in the evening, but
when we arrived in the afternoon to do our sound
check, we discovered that the local hockey team had
refused to allow the ice to be covered. They had a big
game coming up and thought that the concert might
wreck the ice. So our gear was set up at one end of
the rink, the mixing consoles were in the stands, and
the lighting console was on stage with us. Just as we
began sound check, the team started skating around
the rink and practicing. It was very surreal. In the
evening, the crowd was seated at the far end of the
stands and we were playing way down at the other
end because the ice remained uncovered.

If there's an up-side to these near impossible conditions,
it's that they make touring other countries much easier.
Canadian bands are rich in character because they have to
endure interminably long stretches during white-outs on
treacherous highways, pulling together merely to survive
the physical journey. In the U.S., there are millions upon
millions of people waiting to embrace your music, while in
Britain it takes less than an hour to saunter from town to
town. In Canada, you hit Regina and you think, "Whew,
finally a big city!" even though Saskatchewan's capital
would fit three-fold into most American metropolises. I
think that those Canadians who aspire to fame and stay on

ROCK TALK
Along for the Ride

The rock world is not just the domain of musicians. It's also a world of live sound mixers (*soundmen*), road managers (who are responsible for making sure that a gig comes together successfully), drum and guitar *technicians* (folks who are employed to rub and clean and maintain your instrument; I've yet to encounter a bass technician), people who make and sell merchandise (T-shirts, stickers, buttons, hats), bus and van drivers, booking agents (who are responsible for getting you the gig in the first place), lighting technicians, and *roadies*, those unsung yeomen and yeowomen who set up stages and load and unload gear and basically glue the industry together.

top – Bryan Adams, Celine Dion, Alanis Morissette – do so because they've endured the geographic struggle inherent in Canadian rock.

There are certain rules that musicians should heed when heading out on the road. First, there's the food. When Little Feat's great singer and slide guitarist, Lowell George, died, his bandmates explained his death by telling the press that

he'd had one too many road burgers. While this was a
veiled reference to George's drug addiction, they also meant
it in the plain sense that, on the road, you can't help but
return to the burger no matter how hard you try. Not that I
am one, but vegans and vegetarians have the darndest time
trying to maintain their diet, especially when the only
restaurants you have time for are run by guys named
Slappy, whose presence is announced on a neon stick at the
side of a highway. It's hard to finesse your diet on the road,
but if you don't at least try, then the stomach blues will get
you sooner or later. Our second drummer, Don Kerr, was
forever arming himself with little plastic bags filled with
kale and miso and corn chips, which he purchased in cities
for those long trips between health-food stores. As I do
with book and record stores, Don knew the location of
every health-food store in Canada.

After twenty years, the Rheos have become wise to the
routine. We've learned to stop at Blackie's deli while
leaving Victoria, BC, to catch the ferry to the mainland –
which means leaving the hotel thirty minutes early, which
means getting thirty minutes less sleep – as well as
keeping an eye out for Hunky's Perogi Shack outside of
Brandon, Manitoba, or the Hoito in Thunder Bay,
Ontario. I've found that if you discover a decent truck
stop anywhere in Canada, you have to be vigilant about

returning to it, because there are really very few. And even in the good ones, it's best to choose salads and soups over the Tex Mex salsa chicken. You can avoid riskier decisions by making sure there's enough food on hand in the bus or van: corn chips, nuts, and trail mix are all good. Think of yourself as a *coureur de bois* trying to survive for a month in the wilderness, which is pretty much what touring is like anyway.

I'd like to pass on some wisdom regarding touring clothes, etc., but keeping yourself clean is a near impossibility on the road. I suggest that you not fight it and go with the stink. As a rule, bands on the road smell. They're unkempt and foul. The scent of rank footwear and crusted armpits follows young musicians like a creeping fog. Depending on the nature of the gig, your time, in the beginning, will consist of moving from stinking van to stinking club to stinking dressing room to stinking hotel, places that are, sometimes, one and the same. On our first Canadian tour, we played two venues like this: the Royal Albert in Winnipeg, and the National Hotel in Calgary. The minute we arrived at the National, a bedraggled woman came up to Martin and told him not to go into the washroom because her boyfriend was waiting in there to kill him. After seeking refuge in the relative quiet of our rooms, I turned back the sheets to find my pillow stuck to the bed

with dried blood. Another time, a musician I know was
bathing in the communal washroom on the second floor
of the Royal Albert when a disoriented drunk walked in
and peed on his back. No amount of industrial deodorant
is going to keep that sort of thing from happening.

Apart from your instruments, I'd advise that you leave
your valuables at home. A tour is a great repository for lost
things. Even though the Rheos travel on planes these days,
I leave my computer at my desk. This gives me a chance to
write in notebooks (I even brought a suitcase typewriter
with me on one trip), which also gives me a chance to
separate my Home self from my Away self. Touring is a
place where you're forced to be somebody you aren't
anywhere else. You are required to draw on such road-
worthy qualities as instinct, tolerance, endurance,
diplomacy, chastity, and resilience when unleashed into
that great murky Gigland. You learn a lot about coping
beyond your comfort zone, testing your mettle as both an
individual and team player. Will you be able to tolerate the
drunken bass player falling over you while confessing his
deepest fears in the van after the gig, when all you want to
do is sleep? Does it bother you singing into a microphone
that smells of vomit from the last band that used it? How
will you deal with the suspicion that another band
member is getting most of the attention at shows? Are you

uncomfortable being with the same group of people for such a long, intense period of time? Will you object to using a filthy, seatless toilet for the better part of two months? Do you like long drives across vast, empty terrain in closed, airless vehicles with people you're only just starting to know?

Touring means steeling yourself against constant assaults on your character. One of the main differences between being a musician and having a normal job is that criticism doesn't come only from your boss or co-workers, but from yourself. Anxiety and insecurity are two hallmarks of the creative mind, and it's on the road that these qualities are exposed. Every gig is a test of character, of self-worth.

I've witnessed bandmates on the verge of nausea after particularly humiliating performances. The first time we played Pacific Coliseum in Vancouver, we opened for the Barenaked Ladies, the biggest show of our lives after years of touring together. That night, we literally got off on the wrong foot. Our first song was a tough one, "When Winter Comes," that began with Martin playing alone at the foot of the stage. It looked and sounded great, his body soaked in foggy blues, the sound of his guitar filling the cavernous sports bowl while young kids found their seats. But suddenly, things went terribly wrong. Dave Clark was

jaunting across the darkness towards his white drum kit
when he accidentally stepped on a foot pedal, completely
shutting down Martin's guitarworks. Tim and I climbed
onstage into the silence that filled the arena. We stood there,
as cold as snow on an iceberg. I felt like voiding my bowels.
Martin pounded his gear like a caveman taking a rock to a
coconut. Finally, his sound kicked in, but so did the next
forty minutes of misery. It was the worst gig of our lives.

After the show, we pushed our heads into our hands,
wallowing in the crushing disappointment of the occasion.
But as soon as we understood that this was as bad as it
would get, the tragedy of the gig turned into a celebration.
Somebody cracked a beer, told a stupid joke. I grabbed my
guitar from its case and started playing whatever came
into my head. Friends arrived backstage to help balm our
wounded pride, and within hours we'd gone from the
excitement of playing the great hockey rink, to the sorrow
of blowing the gig, to singing at the top of our lungs in the
bowels of the arena. Here was a musician's life wrapped up
in a single day: high to low to high, in extreme measures.
Finally, at two in the morning, security came and asked us
to go home.

Conclusion

A Rage of Light

I've reread everything that you've just finished reading, and I'm left wondering whether or not there's been too much warning in all of these words. After all, I don't want this to be merely a cautionary tale. Lord knows there'll be plenty of that coming from parents, cousins, uncles, guidance counselors, and shop teachers, who, sometimes with good reason, will paint a foreboding picture of the life of a musician. Personally, I want you to get excited so that, if you choose this path, you'll leap into the Life of Rock with both feet. I hope that what I've said hasn't scared you, or instilled any kind of self-doubt. I can say, unequivocally, that rock and roll has given me a better life than I could have imagined. It's through music that I met my girlfriend (now my wife) and closest friends, and because of the pace and tempo of the work – along with the unflagging support of my parents – I'm allowed the freedom to write, which has long been my other passion.

Songwriting and singing and playing guitar gives me the opportunity to make art whenever I have to, whether it's mid-morning or midnight. Musician's hours allow you to engage the muse whenever it strikes; I once wrote a five-minute, nine-part song called "Four Little Songs" after bolting out of slumber in the middle of the night. "Horses," one of my most popular songs, was written the same way. The Angel of Rock knocks and I am able to answer the door. If I had a day job, I doubt this would be the case.

It's through music that I make sense of the greater world, my world, our world. Being a songwriter – any kind of artist, really – demands that you examine what's around you. It forces you to deal with reality, with what your eyes and ears take in. The artist can't simply slide through life, because the public needs him or her to articulate the universal experience, to carve out words and notes when everybody else is sleeping and readying themselves to face the world the next morning. My friend once explained a musician's propensity for ignoring the alarm clock by saying, "We have to keep these hours so that, by eleven o'clock – when the public needs us – we're at our peak ability to perform."

Music is a global passport. Describing my sports books, I've said that, upon wandering into a strange town, the best way to know a place is to find either the local sports team or musicians' haunt. Athletes and musicians beyond all others are accepting of an outside presence. Once, at a train station in Ping Yao – a map dot somewhere on the Chinese plain – I came across a crack-toothed young man in a dirty blue Mao jacket holding what looked like a gourd with a neck and four strings. I sat down beside him on the bench and fished a guitar pick out of my pocket. At first, he had no idea what I was giving him, so I strummed the air. But instead of taking the plectrum, he handed me his instrument. I plucked the quasi-guitar and, within minutes, everyone in the train station was gathered around. The *plink!*ing and *pwauk!*ing echoed around the room as the two of us passed the guitar back and forth. When the train arrived, I tried to give my fellow musician the pick, but he pressed it into my hand, bidding me goodbye in Chinese. He disappeared, bound like Woody Guthrie for the dust of the country's interior.

Once, in Vancouver at the Town Pump nightclub (known disparagingly among locals as the Brown Dump, though I

never found it to be that bad), the Rheostatics were
scheduled to play a show that the promoters had oversold.
There were hundreds of fans waiting to get in, so instead of
offering them a refund, we scheduled a second show. The
first set lasted about two hours. We played great and the
crowd kept calling us back. Afterwards, we looked forward
to enjoying a subdued second show, understanding that
there'd be only a handful of fans in the crowd. But the
promoters had given the audience for the first show the
opportunity to stick around, and they did, so the second
show was even more packed. Surprising ourselves, we took
the performance beyond the dial. It was an intense
physical and emotional experience. The band found an
energy level that we hadn't reached before, hitting one
beautiful moment after another. The gig was the perfect
mix of adrenaline and spirit. All told, we performed five
hours of consecutive, unrelenting Rheo Rock. It was the
greatest concert experience of my life.

There's not a year in which we don't have at least a handful
of these nights, nights when you simply can't stop playing.
All of the other things about being in a rock band – the
politics, the struggle to get above the poverty line, the up
and down nature of the business, one's artistic crisis of
conscience, the fickle nature of the muse – fades into the
fabric when art becomes a rage of light. Mel Brooks, better

known as a comedian, once said, "Every one of my songs is a protest against death." In a life that knocks you around as easily as it draws you close, rock and roll is a cry above the crowd that tells people you're alive. It announces to peers, family, girlfriends, boyfriends, and an ocean of those you'll never know – but who'll know you – that yours is a voice to be heard, no matter the price. Out of tune, rhymed wrong, slope-rhythmed, or chainsaw warm – it doesn't matter. Your voice and your instrument is both a weapon and a tool. What you do with it is who you are.

Acknowledgments

The author – that would be me – would like to thank Kathy Lowinger, Kat Mototsune, and everybody at Tundra Books for helping me make this book. Certain notice should go to Dinah Forbes, my editor at McClelland and Stewart, who walked me down the hallway to Kathy's office. Thanks as well to Dave Johnston, my agent, although he didn't have much to do with this one. This book I thought up all by myself.

The title of the work comes from the AC/DC song "For Those About to Rock (We Salute You)." I considered naming the book after another of their songs – "Dirty Deeds Done Dirt Cheap" – since rock and roll's about that, too. I'd like to thank, with gratitude, everybody whose name I've used here, especially Rheostatics past and present. Cheers as well to all of those fans who've written, called, and occasionally shouted to me across streets; not forgetting Paul Linklater, who contributed to discussions on the art of rock-and-roll tutelage. Also, I'd like to recognize Shauna de Cartier, the Rheostatics' manager, and our . . . um, staff: soundman Steve Clarkson, and technicians Dwayne Gale and Tim Mech. Finally, my love to Janet and the sprogs – Cecilia and Lorenzo. If they're ever required to read this book, I hope they like it. I hope they think that I did okay.

Dave Bidini
Toronto

Please write:
P.O. Box 616
Station C
Toronto, Ontario
M6J 3R9

Index of Musicians and Music